Communications
in Computer and Information Science 1783

Rationale

The CCIS series is devoted to the publication of proceedings of computer science conferences. Its aim is to efficiently disseminate original research results in informatics in printed and electronic form. While the focus is on publication of peer-reviewed full papers presenting mature work, inclusion of reviewed short papers reporting on work in progress is welcome, too. Besides globally relevant meetings with internationally representative program committees guaranteeing a strict peer-reviewing and paper selection process, conferences run by societies or of high regional or national relevance are also considered for publication.

Topics

The topical scope of CCIS spans the entire spectrum of informatics ranging from foundational topics in the theory of computing to information and communications science and technology and a broad variety of interdisciplinary application fields.

Information for Volume Editors and Authors

Publication in CCIS is free of charge. No royalties are paid, however, we offer registered conference participants temporary free access to the online version of the conference proceedings on SpringerLink (http://link.springer.com) by means of an http referrer from the conference website and/or a number of complimentary printed copies, as specified in the official acceptance email of the event.

CCIS proceedings can be published in time for distribution at conferences or as post-proceedings, and delivered in the form of printed books and/or electronically as USBs and/or e-content licenses for accessing proceedings at SpringerLink. Furthermore, CCIS proceedings are included in the CCIS electronic book series hosted in the SpringerLink digital library at http://link.springer.com/bookseries/7899. Conferences publishing in CCIS are allowed to use Online Conference Service (OCS) for managing the whole proceedings lifecycle (from submission and reviewing to preparing for publication) free of charge.

Publication process

The language of publication is exclusively English. Authors publishing in CCIS have to sign the Springer CCIS copyright transfer form, however, they are free to use their material published in CCIS for substantially changed, more elaborate subsequent publications elsewhere. For the preparation of the camera-ready papers/files, authors have to strictly adhere to the Springer CCIS Authors' Instructions and are strongly encouraged to use the CCIS LaTeX style files or templates.

Abstracting/Indexing

CCIS is abstracted/indexed in DBLP, Google Scholar, EI-Compendex, Mathematical Reviews, SCImago, Scopus. CCIS volumes are also submitted for the inclusion in ISI Proceedings.

How to start

To start the evaluation of your proposal for inclusion in the CCIS series, please send an e-mail to ccis@springer.com.

Ulf Brefeld · Jesse Davis · Jan Van Haaren ·
Albrecht Zimmermann
Editors

Machine Learning and Data Mining for Sports Analytics

9th International Workshop, MLSA 2022
Grenoble, France, September 19, 2022
Revised Selected Papers

Editors
Ulf Brefeld
Leuphana University of Lüneburg
Lüneburg, Germany

Jan Van Haaren
KU Leuven
Leuven, Belgium

Jesse Davis ⓘ
KU Leuven
Leuven, Belgium

Albrecht Zimmermann ⓘ
University of Caen Normandy
Caen, France

ISSN 1865-0929   ISSN 1865-0937 (electronic)
Communications in Computer and Information Science
ISBN 978-3-031-27526-5   ISBN 978-3-031-27527-2 (eBook)
https://doi.org/10.1007/978-3-031-27527-2

This Springer imprint is published by the registered company Springer Nature Switzerland AG
The registered company address is: Gewerbestrasse 11, 6330 Cham, Switzerland

Preface

The Machine Learning and Data Mining for Sports Analytics workshop aimed to bring together a diverse set of researchers working on Sports Analytics in a broad sense. In particular, it aimed to attract interest from researchers working on sports from outside of machine learning and data mining. The 9th edition of the workshop was co-located with the European Conference on Machine Learning and Principles and Practice of Knowledge Discovery 2022.

Sports Analytics has been a steadily growing and rapidly evolving area over the last decade, both in US professional sports leagues and in European football leagues. The recent implementation of strict financial fair-play regulations in European football will definitely increase the importance of Sports Analytics in the coming years. In addition, there is the popularity of sports betting. The developed techniques are being used for decision support in all aspects of professional sports, including but not limited to:

- Match strategy, tactics, and analysis
- Player acquisition, player valuation, and team spending
- Training regimens and focus
- Injury prediction and prevention
- Performance management and prediction
- Match outcome and league table prediction
- Tournament design and scheduling
- Betting odds calculation

The interest in the topic has grown so much that there is now an annual conference on Sports Analytics at the MIT Sloan School of Management, which has been attended by representatives from over 70 professional sports teams in eminent leagues such as Major League Baseball, National Basketball Association, National Football League, National Hockey League, Major League Soccer, English Premier League, and the German Bundesliga. Furthermore, sports data providers such as Statsbomb, Stats Perform, and Wyscout have started making performance data publicly available to stimulate researchers who have the skills and vision to make a difference in the sports analytics community. Moreover, the National Football League has been sponsoring a Big Data Bowl where they release data and a concrete question to try to engage the analytics community.

There has been growing interest in the Machine Learning and Data Mining community about this topic, and the 2022 edition of MLSA built on the success of prior editions at ECML PKDD 2013 and ECML PKDD 2015 – ECML/PKDD 2021.

Both the community's on-going interest in submitting to and participating in the MLSA workshop series, and the fact that you are reading the fourth volume of MLSA proceedings show that our workshop has become a vital venue for publishing and presenting sports analytics results. In fact, as participants, many of whom had submitted before, expressed during the workshop itself, venues for presenting machine learning and data mining-based sports analytics work remain rare, motivating us to continue to organize the workshop in future years.

In 2022, the workshop received 18 submissions of which 11 were selected after a single-blind reviewing process involving at least three program committee members per paper. One of the accepted papers was withdrawn from publication in the proceedings; a second one was an extended abstract based on a journal publication. In terms of the sports represented, 2022 saw a return to prior years with soccer making up the majority of submissions, and a slight majority of accepted papers. Topics included tactical analysis, outcome predictions, data acquisition, performance optimization, and player evaluation.

The workshop featured an invited presentation by Stephanie Kovalchik from Zelus Analytics on "Model-based methods for high-performance analysis in sports":

> The how of what makes great athletes great is one of the major topics of sports analytics research. Value attribution is a fundamental tool for quantifying the specific actions and skills that improve outcomes in sport. With the growth in spatial temporal data in high-performance sport, methods for value attribution are becoming increasingly granular and sophisticated. In this talk, I will review several common types of model-based methods for value attribution and present applications in multiple pro sports.

Further information about the workshop can be found on the workshop's website at https://dtai.cs.kuleuven.be/events/MLSA22/.

October 2022   Ulf Brefeld
                                                               Jesse Davis
                                                           Jan Van Haaren
                                                     Albrecht Zimmermann

Organization

Workshop Co-chairs

Ulf Brefeld   Leuphana University, Lüneburg, Germany
Jesse Davis   KU Leuven, Belgium
Jan Van Haaren   Club Brugge, Belgium & KU Leuven, Belgium
Albrecht Zimmermann   Université de Caen Normandie, France

Program Committee

Michael Alcorn   Auburn University, USA
Gennady Andrienko   Fraunhofer, Germany
Swarup Ranjan Behera   Indian Institute of Technology, Guwahati, India
Harish S. Bhat   University of California, USA
Lotte Bransen   SciSports, The Netherlands
Paolo Cintia   University of Pisa, Italy
Arie-Willem de Leeuw   Universiteit Leiden, Belgium
Tom Decroos   Meta, USA
Wouter Duivesteijn   Eindhoven University of Technology, The Netherlands
Martin Eastwood   www.pena.lt/y, UK
Clément Gautrais   Brightclue, France
Kilian Hendrickx   KU Leuven/Siemens Digital Industries Software, Belgium
Mehdi Kaytoue   Infologic, France
Leonid Kholkine   University of Antwerp, Belgium
Stephanie Kovalchik   Zelus Analytics, USA
Patrick Lambrix   Linköping University, Sweden
Jan Lasek   Systems Research Institute, Poland
Laurentius Meerhoff   Leiden Institute of Advanced Computer Science, The Netherlands
Wannes Meert   KU Leuven, Belgium
Luca Pappalardo   University of Pisa, Italy
Konstantinos Pelechrinis   University of Pittsburgh, USA

François Rioult   GREYC CNRS UMR6072 - Université de Caen
                                        Normandie, France
Pieter Robberechts   KU Leuven, Belgium
Maaike Van Roy   KU Leuven, Belgium

Contents

Cycling

Football

Towards Expected Counter - Using Comprehensible Features to Predict Counterattacks

Henrik Biermann[1]([✉])([iD]), Franz-Georg Wieland[2,3]([iD]), Jens Timmer[2,3,4]([iD]), Daniel Memmert[1]([iD]), and Ashwin Phatak[1]([iD])

[1] Institute of Exercise Training and Sport Informatics,
German Sport University of Cologne, Cologne 50933, Germany
`h.biermann@dshs-koeln.de`
[2] Institute of Physics, University of Freiburg, Freiburg, Germany
[3] Freiburg Center for Data Analysis and Modelling (FDM), University of Freiburg,
Freiburg, Germany
[4] Germany Centre for Integrative Biological Signalling Studies (CIBSS),
University of Freiburg, Freiburg, Germany

Abstract. Soccer is a low-scoring game where one goal can make the difference. Thus, counterattacks have been recognized by modern strategy as an effective way to create scoring opportunities from a position of stable defense. This coincidentally requires teams on offense to be mindful of taking risks, i.e. losing the ball. To assess these risks, it is crucial to understand the involved mechanisms that turn ball losses into counterattacks. However, while the soccer analytics community has made progress predicting outcomes of single actions (shots or passes) [1,2] up to entire matches [15], individual sequences like counterattacks have not been predicted with comparable success. In this paper, we give reasons for this and create a framework that allows understanding complex sequences through comprehensible features. We apply this framework to predict counterattacks before they happen. Therefore, we find turnovers in soccer matches and create transparent counterattack labels from spatiotemporal data. Subsequently, we construct comprehensible features from sport-specific assumptions and assess their influence on counterattacks. Finally, we use these features to create a simple binary logistic regression model that predicts counterattacks. Our results show that players behind the ball are the most important predictive factors. We find that if a team loses the ball in the center *and* more than two players are not behind the ball, they concede a counterattack in almost 30% of cases. This stresses the importance to avoid ball losses in build-up play. In the future, we plan to extend this approach to generate more differentiated insights.

Keywords: Soccer analytics · Spatiotemporal data · Event data · Interpretable features

U. Brefeld et al. (Eds.): MLSA 2022, CCIS 1783, pp. 3–13, 2023.
https://doi.org/10.1007/978-3-031-27527-2_1

1   Introduction

As part of a universal language to describe soccer, the so-called moments of play have been introduced. This concept presents a way to organize the sometimes chaotic developments during matches into five phases: The two attacking phases for each team (where the other team defends), two transition phases between these attacking phases, and set pieces [8].

In performance analysis the transition phases have recently gained attention [13]. Counterattacks, i.e. fast attacks after winning the ball from the opposition have been determined as an important factor for goal scoring and chance creation [10,14]. Thus, it is essential for a team's success to investigate potentially dangerous situations for counterattacks. However, existing work rather deals with single actions like passes [1,16] or shots [2] or long-term prediction, i.e. match [15] or competition [7] outcomes. In the mid-term, predictive studies are rare and usually use large feature sets and machine learning which makes it difficult to translate the results into sport-specific insights. Thus, there is a lack of interpretable models that can help to understand the mechanisms involved.

Thus, this study aims to predict counterattacks through comprehensible features. To achieve this, the study proposes a general framework for analyzing complex sequences by building comprehensible features (Sect. 2). It also describes methodological steps by finding turnovers and defining counterattacks (Sect. 3). In Sect. 4 we build comprehensible features and assess their importance for counterattack success, before combining these features into a predictive model in Sect. 5. Section 6 concludes with a summary of our findings and an outlook on future research topics.

2   Framework for Understanding Complex Sequences

Soccer matches are difficult to predict due to the high number of degrees of freedom and lack of structure compared to other sports [11]. Prediction approaches are either done on very small or very large time scales. Short-term approaches aim to predict the outcome of a single event, e.g. expected goals model the success (goal) probability of a given shot [3] and expected passes model the completion probability of a pass [1]. The advantage of such approaches is that it is performed in an enclosed environment (e.g. a particular shot) with a small number of possible outcomes (e.g. goal yes/no). Long-term approaches forecast the outcome of a match [15] or an entire season/tournament [7]. These techniques benefit from compounding the aggregated complexity of individual processes into a small number of outcomes e.g. of the final score or outcome of a match.

Analysis on an intermediate time scale, however, is less frequently approached. This is mainly due to three reasons. (i) Defining clearly defined sequences is difficult. While many colloquial terms like attacking sequence, pressing moment, and counterattack exist, their translation into precise, rule-based definitions is non-trivial. (ii) Even when these situations are characterized, their meaning, importance, and impact in the broader context of the game are not quantified. Thus, defining *success criteria* is difficult as objectives vary, e.g. dependent on playing style or game situation. (iii) Lastly, even if both the sequence and the success criteria are clearly defined, individual sequences comprise a variety of individual (concrete and possible) inherently complex actions.

Fernandez et al. [6] have tackled this problem by developing a framework that estimates the value of a possession at any time using conditional probability and the expected outcome of different possible actions. Their general model can be used to evaluate actions during a sequence, however, it requires exact models for individual actions which may vary between game situations. Bauer et al. [2] have identified pressing situations after turnovers using an XGBoost model and a broad range of hand-crafted features. Their resulting model is highly predictive, however, while the presented relative importance of features offers some insights, this information is not easily translatable to sport-specific terms or guidelines.

Thus, we propose a novel framework to approach the prediction of specific sequences based on comprehensible features. This enables objective and transparent analysis and allows to create concrete questions and actual guidelines.

1. Define a precise, rule-based specification of *sequences of interest*.
2. Define precise, data-driven and sequence-specific *success criteria*.
3. Construct *comprehensible features* based on sequence-specific assumptions.
4. Assess the *prediction capability* of these features for the success of sequences.
5. Build a *predictive model* based on previously identified relevant features.

It is important to note, that the comprehensible features constructed in step three of the process are in general not unique in their ability to predict the sequence success. The complexity of football makes it highly likely, that many different features can be constructed with similar predictive capabilities. This holds especially true, since for any non-trivially constructed feature, many slightly altered features can be found. The choice of feature is thus an integral part of the analysis pipeline, with which the hypothesis space to be examined is already circumscribed. Thus, the feature construction itself already allows for a precise specification of different hypothesis, which also makes it possible to assess the importance of certain feature characteristics by using slightly altered feature subsets in the analysis.

3   Definition of Sequences of Interest and Success Criteria

In this section we introduce rules for identifying *sequences of interest* from turnovers (Sect. 3.1), define a set of sequence-specific *success criteria* for counterattacks (Sect. 3.2), and apply both to create our dataset from a provided number of matches (Sect. 3.3).

3.1   Rule-based Identification of Persistent Open-Play Turnovers

Our provided match data (see Sect. 3.3) contains position and event data of matches, however, lacks information about possession. Thus, we define a turnover

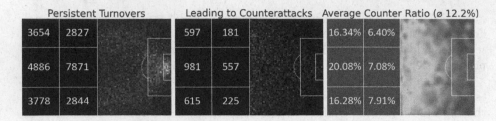

Fig. 1. Influence of location for counterattack probability. Left: Location of *Persistent Turnovers* on the pitch. Middle: Location of *Persistent Turnovers* that turn into counterattacks. Right: Smoothed ratio of counterattacks to total turnovers at every location. For the two left plots the brighter the area the higher the number of occurrences. For the right plot, blue corresponds to low ratios (close to zero) and red regions correspond to high ratios. Dark red corresponds to high ratios up to the maximum value of 40%. Additionally, we divide the pitch into six zones and display the number of turnovers and ratio within a zone. (Color figure online)

as a pair of adjacent events that are assigned to players from opposing teams and refer to the latter as the *ball loss* event. This intuitive definition, however, leads to a large number of turnovers that are not all equally relevant to the present study. Turnovers in the own half of the ball losing team are a special case as they generally involve an immediate attack [2]. Turnovers after set pieces (corner, freekick, throw-in, goalkick, etc.) occur in situations of special (unusual) positioning scenarios [8]. Turnovers that happen during a dead ball (ball-out-of-bounds, foul, offside, etc.) present a special case due to the involved stoppage of play. Finally, turnovers where the ball winning team immediately loses control of the ball (e.g. clearance or a subsequent turnover) indicate that there was no coordinated attack performed. Thus, we exclude the following four subgroups of turnovers:

1. *Own Half Turnover*: The ball at the ball loss event is within the own half of the ball losing team.
2. *Dead Ball Turnover*: Ball loss event is a dead ball.
3. *Set Piece Originated Turnover*: Ball loss event is a set piece or there is a set piece within the last $t_1 = 5$s before the turnover.
4. *Non-persistent Turnover*: After the turnover, there is either another turnover or a dead ball within the next $t_2 = 3$s.

We choose the values for t_1 and t_2 based on discussions with domain experts after watching video material. We exclude the four subsets and refer to the remaining as persistent open-play turnovers in the opposition half, or shorter, *persistent turnovers*. These define the start points of our *sequences of interest*.

3.2 Definition of Success Criteria for Counterattacks

A counterattack has been identified by Lago-Ballesteros et al. [10] as a fast and direct attack (with few players) that starts after winning the ball and by

StatsPerform [12] as a team gaining possession and moving the ball into a target area within the opposition's half (where the speed determines its value). A similarity of both of these definitions is that they include a temporal and a spatial component. Thereupon, we derive the following descriptive *success criteria* for counterattacks:

1. *Spatial*: The distance between the ball and the goal of the ball losing team is reduced to less than $d = 35$ m.
2. *Temporal*: The spatial criterion is met within a time window of $t_3 = 15$ s after the turnover.

However, these definitions do not include possession of a team. Therefore, an uncontrolled clearance (without intent) towards the opponent's half would also be a counterattack. Concerning this, we introduce the additional criterion:

3. *Sustain Possession*: After the spatial criterion is met there is another offensive event (shot, pass, or ball carry) of the ball winning team with a distance of less than $d = 35$ m within the next $t_4 = 5$ s.

The values for d, t_3, and t_4 are carefully chosen after discussion.

3.3   Emerging Dataset

The provided data by Stats Perform contains 289 matches of position data captured 25 Hz and manually captured event data from a recent season of topflight soccer. We exclude all situations where players are missing (e.g. due to a red card). In the remaining data we find 72,367 turnovers (250 per game) of which 18,364 (64 per game, 25.6%) are dead ball turnovers, 8,195 (28, 11.2%) are set piece originated turnovers, 19,948 (69, 27.6%) are non-persistent turnovers and 25,860 (89, 35.6%) are *persistent turnovers*. In the set of *persistent turnovers*, we find 3,156 (11 per game, 12.2%) turnovers that turn into a counterattack. We divide the pitch into a grid of $1m^2$ squares and use the location of turnovers and counterattack labels to compute the ratio of counterattacks to total turnovers at each location. We perform a smoothing of the ratio according to [9] with smoothing factor of $s = 2.5$. The number of turnovers and counterattacks in the grid and the ratio of counterattacks are visualized in Fig. 1.

4   Comprehensible Features for Prediction

In this section we make domain-specific assumptions about favorable scenarios during counterattacks to construct three distinct *comprehensible features* (Sect. 4.1). Subsequently, we reflect on the influence of the ball loss location (Sect. 4.2). Finally, we assess each feature's capability to predict counterattacks by comparing counterattack ratios for specific values with the average ratio (Sects. 4.3).

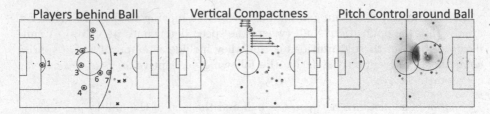

Fig. 2. Computation of the three constructed interpretable features for an exemplary turnover situation. Displayed are the positions of the ball (black), the ball losing team (purple), and the ball winning team (orange). Left: Losing players behind ball are circled. Middle: The vertical distance of the circled player to all teammates is indicated. Right: Pitch control surface [5] with exponentially decreasing weights around the ball is shown and the most relevant area for computing pitch control is circled. (Color figure online)

4.1   Constructing Features from Domain-Specific Assumptions

As discussed in Sect. 2 the features constructed below are not unique and slight variation of these features can as well be used with comparable results. Therefore, we try to report our specific domain-specific assumptions on which the features are based while also discussing some related features that could have been used.

We generally assume that having many players to defend is beneficial for the ball losing team [4]. However, due to the direct and fast nature [10] of counterattacks, it may be difficult for some players that were previously on offense to do so. Thus, we estimate whether a player is able to defend against a possible counterattack by comparing its position with the position of the ball. Therefore, we count all players with less distance to the losing team's goal than the ball and refer to this feature as *losing players behind ball*.

This feature is related to the number of ball winning players behind the ball. These players will be in an ideal position to conduct the counter attack. Furthermore, the ratio or difference between losing and ball winning players behind the ball could also be assessed. Choosing *losing players behind ball* thus emphasises the importance of defending and decelerating counter attacks with numbers over the numerical balance or attacking player number during the counter attack.

Moreover, we presume that a compact defensive shape closes free spaces on the pitch and, thus, limits the possibilities for the attacking team. Vertical compactness is assumed to be especially effective [4]. In its simplest form, a compact shape can be viewed as a dense formation with small distances between players. Thus, we compute the average vertical distance between fieldplayers of the ball losing team and refer to this feature as the *losing vertical compactness*.

The horizontal compactness of the ball losing team is a related feature to its vertical compactness. By focusing on vertical compactness, the assumption is that counter attacks are much less likely to succeed, if the team has moved up the pitch cohesively and has small distances between the players vertically. This usually implies, that the opponent has had to move back as well to defend the cohesive attack.

Finally, we assume that controlling space around the ball is beneficial for defense as it may prevent progress of the ball winning team [4]. We, thus, compute space occupation for every pitch location using the approach from Fernandez et al. [5]. To value spaces around the ball we use an exponentially decreasing function of the ball distance with decay parameter $\alpha = 0.2$. This decay parameter is equivalent to a half-distance of the space control of $3.5m$, which means that a player 3.5 m away from the ball contributes half as much as a player directly positioned on the ball. We aggregate the space occupation for both teams into a single value by choosing a negative sign for the ball winning team. Thus, we refer to this value as *losing pitch control* since it corresponds with spatial dominance of the losing ball team.

4.2 Influence of Ball Loss Location for Feature Assessment

The ratio of counterattacks (see Fig. 1) reveals a strong influence of the ball loss location for counterattack probability. Turnovers in the pitch center have a higher probability to become counterattacks than turnovers closer to the winning team's goal. This is likely caused by the lower distance that needs to be overcome within a given time to count as a counterattack (see Sect. 3.2).

However, this influence needs to be included in the assessment of features. All three constructed features correlate with ball loss location to some degree. Therefore, they already possess some predictive power that does not stem from their tactical relevance. Thus, we do not evaluate overall counterattack probability but rather the derivation to the average ratio at a location (see Fig. 1). Hence, to gain an impression of prediction capability, we employ feature-specific thresholds that were chosen to separate the set of *persistent turnovers* into two comparably large but also distinct subsets. We group all turnovers with feature values below the threshold into one group and all turnovers with values above the threshold into another group. For both subsets, we compute individual counterattack ratios for every pitch location (as presented in Sect. 3.3). Finally, we respectively subtract the average counterattack ratio to obtain differences.

4.3 Prediction Capability of the Constructed Features

Losing Players Behind Ball. We choose a threshold of eight players and yield two comparably sized subsets (see Fig. 3). The differences to the average ratios display a largely increased probability for below-threshold turnovers. This effect is especially valid in the pitch center while a low number of turnovers near the corner flags influences the results.

Losing Vertical Compactness. In this case, we choose a threshold of 13m to create two distinct subsets (see Fig. 4). The differences to average ratio show a small zone-dependent effect of *vertical compactness*. The below-threshold turnovers

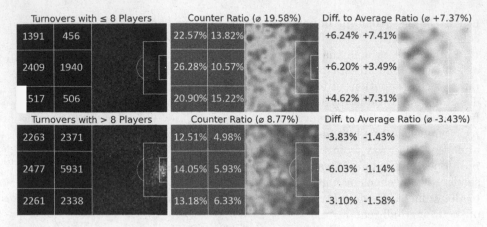

Fig. 3. Influence of *losing players behind ball* for counterattacks. Left: Number of turnovers. Middle: Ratio of counterattacks. Right: Difference to the average counter-attack ratio (Fig. 1). Top row: Below-threshold turnovers with eight or less players. Bottom row: Above-threshold turnovers with at least nine players. For the right plot, we choose green for values below and pink for values above location average. The maximum value is ±15%. (Color figure online)

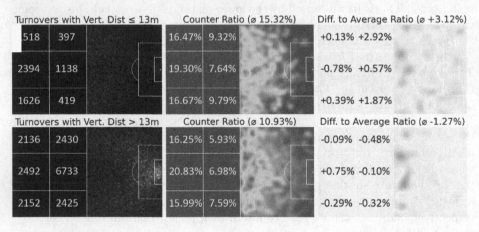

Fig. 4. Influence of *losing compactness* for counterattacks. Top row: Compactness up to 13m. Bottom row: Compactness of more than 13 m. For full caption see Fig. 3.

(good *vertical compactness*) have a slightly decreased probability of a counterattack in the pitch center. For zones near the sidelines, however, this effect is not observable. Yet again, the zones near the corner flags show a considerably small number of below-threshold turnovers which might influence the results.

Pitch Control around the Ball. We create subsets using a feature threshold of -0.35 (see Fig. 5). A negative threshold was chosen to obtain comparable sizes as the ball winning team naturally controls more space in the majority of cases.

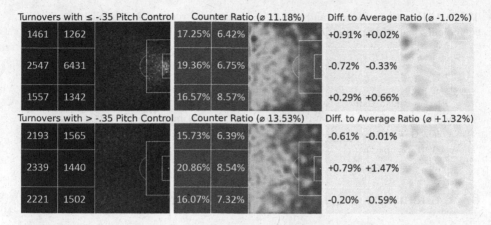

Turnovers with ≤ -.35 Pitch Control		Counter Ratio (ø 11.18%)		Diff. to Average Ratio (ø -1.02%)
1461	1262	17.25%	6.42%	+0.91% +0.02%
2547	6431	19.36%	6.75%	-0.72% -0.33%
1557	1342	16.57%	8.57%	+0.29% +0.66%
Turnovers with > -.35 Pitch Control		Counter Ratio (ø 13.53%)		Diff. to Average Ratio (ø +1.32%)
2193	1565	15.73%	6.39%	-0.61% -0.01%
2339	1440	20.86%	8.54%	+0.79% +1.47%
2221	1502	16.07%	7.32%	-0.20% -0.59%

Fig. 5. Influence of *losing pitch control* for counterattacks. Top row: Pitch control of -0.35 or less. Bottom row: Pitch control of more than -.35. For full caption see Fig. 3.

The results indicate ambiguous influence of pitch control on counterattack probability. Above threshold turnovers (good *losing pitch control*) show a slightly decreased probability of a counterattack for zones near the sidelines. However, they also show a slightly increased probability of a counterattack at the pitch center. This is likely because good occupation of spaces around the ball correlates with the poor occupation of spaces away from the ball. Thus, this effect might describe failed pressing attempts of the ball losing team to some degree.

5   Model-based Test of Features

We test our set of comprehensible features in a predictive logistic regression model with balanced class weights. To incorporate the influence of location we use the direct distance to the losing team's goal additionally to the three constructed features. A binary Logistic regression with '12' regularization was performed using the handcrafted features (see Table 1) as independent variables. The model was further evaluated using five-fold cross-validation which was performed in order to check the out-of-sample validity. Furthermore, feature coefficients and their respective odds ratios were computed to assess the influence of the features. The results show that losing players behind ball had the highest (negative) influence on counterattacks. Pitch control shows the second-highest influence in predicting a successful counterattack. The goal distance and losing vertical compactness show negligible effects. The results of the 5-fold cross validation display a general capability of the model to predict counterattacks. Small deviance between individual splits indicates the stability of the model. However, the absolute values still show room for improvement.

Table 1. Feature influences and results of the logistic regression model. Left: Feature coefficients and odds ratio (OR). Right: Cross-validation results for different metrics.

Feature	Coeff.	OR		Metric	Cross-val results
Intercept	4.285	72.591		F1-Weighted	0.6417 ± 0.0029
Los. Players Behind Ball	-0.218	0.804		AUC	0.6916 ± 0.0037
Losing Pitch Control	-0.150	0.860		Accuracy	0.6418 ± 0.0029
Los. Team Goal Distance	-0.027	0.973		Recall	0.6532 ± 0.0077
Losing Vert. Compactness	-0.008	0.993			

6   Conclusion

We have made a first approach towards an exhaustive expected counter metric. Using our proposed framework for understanding complex sequences we have created a dataset of *sequences of interest* with counterattacks labels based on intuitive *success criteria*. We have constructed three comprehensible features for counterattack success and assessed the prediction capability of the features using manually defined threshold values. Based on the features we created a simple predictive logistic regression model. The framework has revealed various comprehensible insights in how to prevent counterattacks. Most prominently, players behind the ball are highly important for preventing counterattacks. Thus, players in the back need to avoid turnovers (e.g. during build-up play) as much as possible. More space control is also beneficial to prevent counterattacks, especially at the sidelines. Less significant, a vertical compact shape is beneficial in the center. Our model predicts the risk of a turnover with substantial performance. Thus, it can be employed for various sport-specific applications (e.g. evaluate tactical fouls or create risk-reward profiles). Admittedly, the assessment with hand-defined thresholds does not capture fine-grained statistical anomalies in feature distributions. Moreover, our model depends on choices influencing the dataset (*sequences of interest*) and features. Thus, in future we plan to carefully evaluate these choices and to incorporate more sophisticated continous *success criteria* [6]. Finally, our approach may benefit from a larger dataset. However, due to the detailed insights gained on the matter of counterattacks we promote our framework for analyzing all types of complex sequences in soccer (e.g. build-up play or different set pieces).

Acknowledgements. This research was supported by a grant from the German Research Council (DFG) to DM (grant ME 2678/30.1).

References

1. Anzer, G., Bauer, P.: Expected passes: determining the difficulty of a pass in football (soccer) using spatio-temporal data. Data Min. Knowl. Disc. **36**(1), 295–317 (2022). https://doi.org/10.1007/s10618-021-00810-3. https://link.springer.com/10.1007/s10618-021-00810-3

2. Bauer, P., Anzer, G.: Data-driven detection of counterpressing in professional football: a supervised machine learning task based on synchronized positional and event data with expert-based feature extraction. Data Min. Knowl. Disc. **35**(5), 2009–2049 (2021). https://doi.org/10.1007/s10618-021-00763-7. https://link.springer.com/10.1007/s10618-021-00763-7

3. Bauer, P., Anzer, G.: A goal scoring probability model for shots based on synchronized positional and event data in football (soccer). Front. Sports Active Living **3**, 53 (2021). https://doi.org/10.3389/fspor.2021.624475

4. Fernandes, T., Camerino, O., Garganta, J., Pereira, R., Barreira, D.: Design and validation of an observational instrument for defence in soccer based on the Dynamical Systems Theory. Int. J. Sports Sci. Coach. **14**(2), 138–152 (2019). https://doi.org/10.1177/1747954119827283. http://journals.sagepub.com/doi/10.1177/1747954119827283

5. Fernandez, J., Bornn, L.: Wide Open Spaces: a statistical technique for measuring space creation in professional soccer. In: Sloan sports analytics conference, vol. 2018 (2018)

6. Fernández, J., Bornn, L., Cervone, D.: A framework for the fine-grained evaluation of the instantaneous expected value of soccer possessions. Mach. Learn. **110**(6), 1389–1427 (2021). https://doi.org/10.1007/s10994-021-05989-6. https://link.springer.com/10.1007/s10994-021-05989-6

7. Groll, A., Schauberger, G., Tutz, G.: Prediction of major international soccer tournaments based on team-specific regularized Poisson regression: an application to the FIFA World Cup 2014. J. Quant. Anal. Sports **11**(2), 97–115 (2015). https://doi.org/10.1515/jqas-2014-0051. https://www.degruyter.com/document/doi/10.1515/jqas-2014-0051/html

8. Hewitt, A., Greenham, G., Norton, K.: Game style in soccer: what is it and can we quantify it? Int. J. Perform. Anal. Sport **16**(1), 355–372 (2016)

9. Hockeyviz: Smoothing: how to (2022). https://hockeyviz.com/howto/smoothing

10. Lago-Ballesteros, J., Lago-Peñas, C., Rey, E.: The effect of playing tactics and situational variables on achieving score-box possessions in a professional soccer team. J. Sports Sci. **30**(14), 1455–1461 (2012)

11. Liu, G., Luo, Y., Schulte, O., Kharrat, T.: Deep soccer analytics: learning an action-value function for evaluating soccer players. Data Min. Knowl. Disc. **34**(5), 1531–1559 (2020). https://doi.org/10.1007/s10618-020-00705-9

12. LLC, S.: Playing Styles Definition by StatsPerform (2022). https://www.statsperform.com/resource/stats-playing-styles-introduction/

13. Memmert, D., Raabe, D.: Data analytics in football: positional data collection, modelling and analysis. Routledge, Abingdon, Oxon; 1 edn. New York, NY : Routledge (2018). https://doi.org/10.4324/9781351210164. https://www.taylorfrancis.com/books/9781351210157

14. Raudonius, L., Allmendinger, R.: Evaluating football player actions during counterattacks. In: Yin, H., et al. (eds.) IDEAL 2021. LNCS, vol. 13113, pp. 367–377. Springer, Cham (2021). https://doi.org/10.1007/978-3-030-91608-4_36

15. Robberechts, P., Van Haaren, J., Davis, J.: A Bayesian approach to in-game win probability in soccer. In: Proceedings of the 27th ACM SIGKDD Conference on Knowledge Discovery & Data Mining, pp. 3512–3521 (2021). https://doi.org/10.1145/3447548.3467194. http://arxiv.org/abs/1906.05029. arXiv: 1906.05029

16. Spearman, W.R., Basye, A.T., Dick, G.J., Hotovy, R., Hudl, P.P.: Physics-based modeling of pass probabilities in soccer (2017)

Shot Analysis in Different Levels of German Football Using Expected Goals

Laurynas Raudonius[1]([⊠]) and Thomas Seidl[2]

[1] ETH Zürich, Rämistrasse 101, 8092 Zürich, Switzerland
lraudonius@student.ethz.ch
[2] VfB Stuttgart, 1893 AG, Mercedesstraße 109, 70372 Stuttgart, Germany
T.Seidl@vfb-stuttgart.de

Abstract. Shooting has been one of the most analyzed and researched parts of association football as it directly leads to goals which determine the score of the match. We take a look at it from a previously unseen perspective and analyze if there are differences between four different levels in German football (Bundesliga, Regionalliga, U19 Bundesliga and U17 Bundesliga) in shooting tendencies and efficiency and explore how these change as players get older. To do that we employ statistical analysis and examine the individual weights of Expected Goals models based on logistic regression. We find that players in higher levels tend to be more risky and aim for corners of the goal and are more predictable in terms of their shot origins. A comparison of headers and kicks show that goal likelihood of the latter is much more influenced by whether a shot has happened after a set piece, whereas goal likelihood of headers decreases more steeply with increasing distance from goal. Analysis also reveals that with increasing level goalkeepers tend to be more reliable saving shots at medium height but have a harder time with shots aimed at bottom corners.

Keywords: Football analytics · Sports analytics · Performance analysis · Machine learning · Expected goals

1 Introduction

Johan Cruyff, a Dutch footballer and manager widely regarded as one of the greatest in the history of the sport, once famously said "You have to shoot, otherwise you can't score". And really, just following a very basic deduction, the result of a football match is determined solely by goals scored, and in most cases these are a direct result of shots.

The importance of these particular events occurring in a football match can be proven not only by common sense, but also by historical data, as the number of total shots per match was found to be among the best differentiators between winning and losing teams [7]. Combining this with the shots being relatively basic events, it is no surprise that they are among the most widely researched events among academics in the football analytics field [3,9,10].

Supported by VfB Stuttgart.

Following this, arguably the most popular regression model in football analytics field called Expected Goals was produced. The model is trained on historical data; it takes shot information such as distance from goal, angle, body part etc. and returns a single number - the likelihood of that shot ending in the back of the net. Expected Goals gained traction in the past decade and is now the core philosophy behind Brentford's successful push for a spot in the Premier League [19]. We will be using our own Expected Goals models and examine their weights to explore differences between different types of shots in four leagues of German football - Bundesliga, Regionalliga, U19 Bundesliga and U17 Bundesliga. As each of the leagues has a higher average player age than the level below (see Fig. 1), we will also explore how shooting tendencies and success rates change as players grow older and play in higher levels.

2 Related Work

Even though right now there are no particular works that focused on changes in shooting tendencies as footballers get older, there has been some research done on the effects of aging to the psychology of both professional athletes and the general population. Among works on the latter, various studies have found that generally, the tendency to take risks declines with age [5,17] - one of the proposed causes for that is cognitive aging, but it does not influence the decisions until people are 50+ years old and the difference between, for example, 18 and 35 year olds is not overly noticeable.

A considerable amount of research has been carried out on the effect of age on the physicality and psychology of athletes. A work by Rábano-Muñoz et al. found that there is a large difference between physical demands in under 17 and under 19 year old small-sided football games, with U19 level being even more physically demanding than senior player (aged 20 and over) level [18]. Interestingly, similar results were observed by Benítez-Sillero et al., this time focusing on the psychology of players of different age levels [4]. Players in the U19 level again scored the highest (even compared to older players) in various mental metrics including motivation, attitude control, attention control etc. Somewhat contradictory, Trninić et al. conducted a study that found older athletes in team sports to be more agreeable, conscientious (able to control emotions and impulses) and all around, stable [20]. Staying focused on football, the position of the player also can be taken into account, as players in different positions seem to peak at different ages [24].

As mentioned in the introduction, shots are among the most researched events in football analytics, both by scientists and analytics enthusiasts alike. Most of the studies revolve around Expected Goals, a Machine Learning (mostly regression, but recently Artificial Neural Networks have been used as well) model that produces the likelihood of a shot resulting in a goal based on historical data. The idea was first introduced by Richard Pollard and Charles Reep (widely regarded as the first football analyst) in 1997, their logistic regression model had distance and angle from goal, whether the player touched the ball before shooting, whether the shot was pressured and whether it happened after a set

16   L. Raudonius and T. Seidl

piece as features [14]. A study that followed found distance to goal and to the nearest defender to be the most important variables that help predict whether a shot will be successful [13]. A surprisingly accurate model that predicted Premier League and Bundesliga shot likelihoods only took distance and angle from goal as features [15]. On the other end of the spectrum, football data providers nowadays have highly complex Expected Goals models with numerous features such as goalkeeper position or ball height at the time of impact - in some cases their models are no longer even based on regression [1,22,23].

3   Methodology

As mentioned in the introduction, we will first analyze the statistics between the four leagues and then examine the performance of Expected Goals models with different designs.

3.1   Data

The analysis is based on anonymized event data collected by Wyscout and consisted of shots from 2020/2021 and 2021/2022 seasons in four different German football leagues[1], general facts one these can be found in Table 1. While U17 and U19 Bundesligas have constraints on player age, in Regionalliga there are many reserve teams with younger players. Those particular four leagues were selected as they are a somewhat general pathway for players from academies: going from U17s to U19s, to reserves and finally to Bundesliga, with each representing a next level of German football pyramid.

Table 1. Facts of the four leagues.

	Bundesliga	Regionalliga	U19 League	U17 League
Tier	1st	4th	1st for U19s	1st for U17s
ø-Age	25.9	24.7	18.5	16.9
No. of matches	597	949	509	573
No. of shots	13461	19844	11617	12213

Every shot in the dataset has the following attributes [2,12]:

- X and Y coordinates
- body part qualifier
- whether the shot was after a set piece
- whether the shot was on target
- whether the shot resulted in a goal
- what part of the goal did the shot go in

---

[1] Some matches were missing from the datasets as they were cancelled or not yet recorded, hence the odd number of matches in leagues.

3.2   Statistical Analysis

Across the four leagues, we will analyse general trends, differences in frequency of shot destinations, shot origins and goalkeeper performance with respect to different zones in the goal. Additionally, we will use analysis of variance (ANOVA) to investigate if the leagues differ significantly.

3.3   Expected Goals Models

Design Considerations. As mentioned in the literature review, state of the art Expected Goals models are highly complex, have numerous features and sometimes replace regression with neural network as the base model, which in turn no longer allows them to examine individual weights to explore the effect each parameter has on the goal probability. This is all done to achieve highest possible accuracy, also noteworthy is that robust training is made possible by large amounts of historical data. As our ultimate goal isn't perfect accuracy and we have access to a limited amount of data, we have gone a different direction.

Our models are quite simplistic as we have sacrificed some of the accuracy to prevent possible overfitting and obtain robust models that could provide some general insights into how the effect of variables changes based on league. Another argument for simple models is the amount of data we have - according to research, for a robust complex model data from at least five seasons might be necessary [16], and sadly we don't have that luxury. Since we want to examine actual weights of the models, we will separate them in two parts - one for foot shots and one for headers. A single model could be tailored to accommodate both types of shots using dummy variables [8], however it would likely make weight examination cluttered.

Model. As logistic regression is a model most widely used to predict the probability of one event taking place (in our case the event is goal), we decided to use it for both models. The particular implementation to obtain the models was R's Generalized Linear Model (*glm* command), it was trained on 80% and tested on the remaining 20% of the shots and did not use regularization as we want to examine individual weights. Following other works on Expected Goals [13–15], we transformed X and Y coordinates to distance from the center of the goal and angle from the center of the goal in radians. Since in the general statistics shot success in all leagues seemed to be heavily influenced by whether the shot was a result of a set piece, it was also included as a parameter for our models. As we do not really have any more information on the goals, these three numbers will serve as our features, it also leaves us with relatively simple models to examine the weights of. You can find the mathematical definition of our model in Eq. 1. Because for both models we have the same features, they are defined exactly the same way - they will just be trained on different data.

$$G(x) = \frac{1}{1 + e^{-(\beta_0 + \beta_1 * x_{distance} + \beta_2 * x_{angle} + \beta_3 * x_{isSetPiece})}} \tag{1}$$

4   Results

4.1   Statistical Analysis

Analysis of Variance. Using ANOVA we found that the shot distances vary significantly between leagues ($p_{value} < 2 * 10^{-16}$), whereas goal zone efficiencies and frequencies and shot origin frequencies do not seem to be significantly different in different levels ($p_{value} > 0.05$). However, we can still examine individual numbers of these to extract minor patterns.

Table 2. General statistics of the four leagues.

Measure	Bundesliga	Regionalliga	U19 League	U17 League
Shots	13461	19844	11617	12213
Goals	1594	2355	1531	1737
Shots per match	22.55	20.91	22.82	21.31
Goals per match	2.67	2.48	3.01	3.03
Goals per shot	0.12	0.12	0.13	0.14
Saved shots, %	25.67%	26.27%	26.40%	27.72%
Off-target shots, %	62.69%	62.08%	60.73%	58.43%
On-target shots saved, %	68.56%	69.06%	66.92%	66.20%
Headers, %	17.44%	15.47%	13.59%	13.98%
Header success rate	0.13	0.13	0.15	0.16
Left foot shots, %	31.73%	31.14%	32.59%	31.97%
Left foot shot success rate	0.11	0.11	0.12	0.14
Right foot shots, %	50.83%	53.39%	53.82%	54.06%
Right foot shot success rate	0.12	0.12	0.14	0.14
Penalty box shots, %	64.12%	61.54%	60.02%	60.27%
Penalty box shot success rate	0.16	0.17	0.19	0.20
Shots from set pieces, %	20.57%	22.31%	20.95%	21.98%
Set pieces success rate	0.10	0.11	0.12	0.14
Average distance, m (shots)	17.21	17.58	18.09	17.89
Average distance, m (goals)	12.02	11.75	12.63	12.57

General Statistics and Shot Destinations. Looking through the general statistics that can be found in Table 2, there are both some expected results which we have anticipated and unexpected findings which contradict our prior hypotheses. With Bundesliga being the highest level of the four, we knew it was a physical league (especially compared to U17 and U19 levels), so it having the biggest share of headers should not surprise anyone too much. Similarly to the percentage of shots that are taken within the penalty box - at the highest level of German football we expected the players to take the best quality chances.

On the other hand, there are some findings that, at least initially, raised our eyebrows. For one, with Bundesliga players obviously being of the highest level and, likely, more ambidextrous than younger ones, we expected a larger share of left foot shots there, when in reality the scores between leagues are very much similar. Another unexpected result was the success rates of every single type of shot decreasing as the players got older, with Bundesliga players being the least efficient. Adding to that, we certainly did not expect them to on average have the most off target shots of the four leagues. Let's explore this counter-intuitive phenomenon further.

One possible explanation for that is that the tempo of the game is a lot higher in higher levels and players don't have that much time to prepare an accurate shot. To add to that, we can also take a look at where the shots actually went - for example, let's examine the difference between Bundesliga (Fig. 1a) and U17 League (Fig. 1b), as the difference in Shot off target % is the largest between these two. There is a substantial difference in what share of the shots are aimed towards the middle, which generally is the least challenging portion of the goal for the goalkeeper. This particular part of goal is more favoured by the young players and even though it does count as a shot on target, the expected return from it is quite small. Players in the 1st tier, on the other hand, chose the sides of the goal more frequently, the difference is most noticeable in the top corners, which unsurprisingly are the most efficient shot destinations if the player is able to guide the ball there, especially with the goalkeepers getting better in higher levels. The effectiveness of such a decision is also backed up by research which suggests that in order to score efficiently, players should aim very close to the inside post [21].

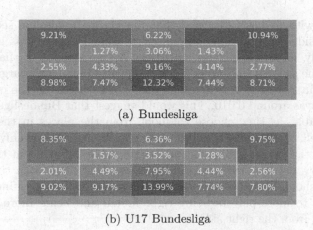

(a) Bundesliga

(b) U17 Bundesliga

Fig. 1. Differences in shot destinations between leagues.

Shot Origin. Now that we've covered shot destinations, let's look into where the shots came from in the four leagues - the frequency heatmaps can be found in Fig. 2[2]. For this, the final third of the pitch was divided in 2×2 meter squares, similarly to a proposition already observed in research on dangerousity in football [11].

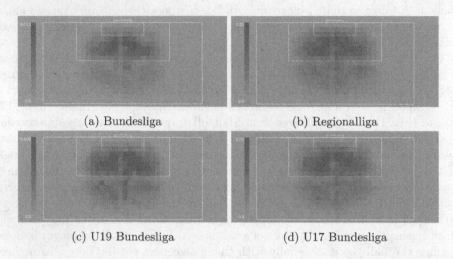

(a) Bundesliga   (b) Regionalliga

(c) U19 Bundesliga   (d) U17 Bundesliga

Fig. 2. Differences in shot locations between leagues. The frequency of the location corresponds to the color of the square, with most frequent locations being colored solid red. (Color figure online)

To begin with, it has to be said that players in Bundesliga seem to shoot less from outside the box than players from other leagues. This is backed up by the already discussed general statistics. A consequence of that is that in Bundesliga, the squares that are inside the penalty box have a larger frequency - the maximum observed in Bundesliga was 0.013 whereas in the other leagues that number was around 0.010. This would suggest that Bundesliga players are more predictable, as they choose to shoot from the places in the pitch they know very well, while shots from younger players are more evenly distributed in that respect. One more phenomenon that can be observed in the graphs is the asymmetry between left and right parts of the pitch, with the right side having more shots in each of the leagues. This, although interesting, can easily be attributed to more players being right footed and being more comfortable with shooting from the right side.

---

[2] The column to the left of the penalty mark and the row below penalty box being considerably less intense than their neighbours is attributed to limitations in the data as shot positions are represented as integers. The column and row in question have only two possible y-positions associated with it while their neighboring rows and columns have three positions, therefore these particular two have less recorded shots.

Goalkeeper Performance. The last thing we will cover in this section is performance of the goalkeepers in the different leagues. The most important part of the general statistics table for this is the 'On-target shots saved, %' row. From this we can see that there is a relatively significant disconnect between two leagues with higher average age and two youth leagues, with goalkeepers at the higher level saving a bigger share of shots they face.

We can examine their performance faced with shots heading into different parts of the goal as well in Fig. 3. The first very obvious thing is that the top corners are the worst zones for the goalkeeper to concede a shot in, shots that end up in there have 30-40% more chance to end up in a goal than, for example, shots straight to the middle of a goal. This in a way backs up the already discussed tendency of Bundesliga players to aim for the top corners even if the probability of missing the target is large.

Another tendency of the goalkeepers is that the ability to save shots at medium height seems to increase with age quite linearly, with goalkeepers at every level being better there than their counterparts on level below. On the other hand, bottom corners are zones that display an opposite trend - except for goalkeepers in Regionalliga, the ones playing in a higher level seem to have a harder time saving shots to bottom corners than the ones playing at U17 or U19 level.

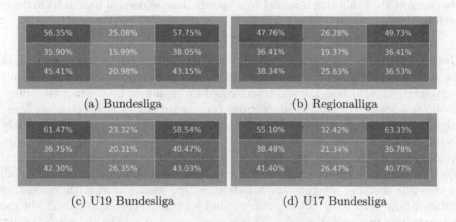

(a) Bundesliga   (b) Regionalliga

(c) U19 Bundesliga   (d) U17 Bundesliga

Fig. 3. Differences in success rate for different zones in goal across the leagues. Most efficient locations are colored solid red. (Color figure online)

4.2 Expected Goals Models

Performance. In order to examine individual weights of the trained models, we first must be sure that we have models that are accurate. To check that, we compared the performance of our models on unseen shots against performance of wyscout's Expected Goals model which we treated as the baseline. We have chosen Brier score as our performance measure [6] because in comparison to

AUROC it punishes uncalibrated models and has been used to evaluate Expected Goals models in the past [16].

Surprisingly, our model was even able to slightly outperform wyscout's in some cases and all around had a very similar performance to the baseline. The full scores can be found in Table 3.

Table 3. Brier score comparison between our and wyscout models accross the leagues. Smaller Brier Score suggests better performance.

League	Headers		Kicks	
	Our	Wyscout	Our	Wyscout
Bundesliga	0.086	0.091	0.088	0.086
Regionalliga	0.096	0.098	0.090	0.087
U19 League	0.111	0.111	0.095	0.091
U17 League	0.131	0.128	0.099	0.096

Since our models have very similar performance to the baseline, we can examine individual weights and expect to find meaningful results. These differences also suggest that tailoring a model to a specific league does not seem to make it perform better, which is also backed up by research [16].

General Insights. A very obvious and quite surprising result was that in all of the 8 models (2 models * 4 leagues), the angle was found to be an insignificant parameter. This, although unexpected, could be explained by the fact that players do not really attempt to shoot from very acute angles that often, so there might not be enough data for the model to deduce that those types of shot rarely go in.

Aside from the angle, every model recognized the intercept, distance and whether the shot was the result of a set piece as significant variables. In all models the distance weights are negative, which means that with increasing distance from goal while holding other variables constant, the probability of the shot resulting in a goal decreases. This is very much expected and quite obvious.

On a more interesting note, all set piece weights are also negative, which means that a shot being a result of a set piece reduces the goal likelihood as well if other variables don't change. Before carrying out the project we could not really anticipate this, but, after examining the general statistics and seeing that shots from set pieces are indeed less likely to end up in the back of the net than other shots, this makes sense.

Headers. The trained model weights for headed shots can be found in Table 4.

Taking a look in the particular values in distance weights, there seems to be a disconnect between the first three leagues and the U17 Bundesliga. In U17 level

Table 4. Weights of the header model across the leagues.

League	Intercept	Distance weight	Set piece weight
Bundesliga	0.60	−0.26	−0.27
Regionalliga	0.50	−0.26	−0.13
U19 League	0.78	−0.26	−0.22
U17 League	0.65	−0.22	−0.39

Table 5. Weights of the foot shot model across the leagues.

League	Intercept	Distance weight	Set piece weight
Bundesliga	0.81	−0.17	−0.68
Regionalliga	0.96	−0.18	−0.53
U19 League	0.98	−0.17	−0.59
U17 League	0.81	−0.16	−0.46

the goal likelihood seems to be somewhat less connected to distance from goal than elsewhere. Looking at the set piece weights, the magnitude of those has to be taken into account - set pieces seem to have three times as much influence on the Expected Goals from headers in the U17 League than in Regionalliga.

Kicked Shots. The trained model weights for foot shots can be found in Table 5.

Examining the intercept values, it seems that Regionalliga and U19 Bundesliga players are in general better at converting shots with their feet than their counterparts in Bundesliga and U17 Bundesliga. Similar to headers, the U17 Bundesliga shots seem to be the least affected by increasing distance from goal, whereas in Regionalliga goal likelihood decreases most rapidly with an increase in distance.

Comparison Between Headers and Kicks. Comparing the values between the header and foot shot models, we can first observe that distance from goal seems to have a bigger negative effect to headers than to kicks. This is very much expected and intuitive, as headers tend to be scored from closer range, moving the player away from the goal while holding other variables constant then decreases the goal likelihood more drastically. A more interesting phenomenon can be examined in the intercept and set piece weights. Even though from general statistics we found that headers are a more efficient shot type than kicks in all leagues, foot shot models from all leagues having larger intercepts seem to contradict that. However, set piece weights cannot be forgotten, and these are also larger in magnitude than the header shots, but negative. If we combine the two pieces of information, it no longer contradicts the general statistics, but rather tells us that whether a shot happened after a set piece has a 3 times larger negative effect on the goal likelihood to kicks than it does to headers.

After analysis of variance (ANOVA) we found that header ($p_{value} = 4.24 *$
10^{-12}) and kicked shot ($p_{value} < 2 * 10^{-16}$) Expected Goal values from our
models varied significantly between the four leagues - the distributions can be
observed in Appendix A.

5   Conclusions

In this work we analysed and presented differences between four football leagues
in Germany (Bundesliga, Regionalliga, U19 Bundesliga and U17 Bundesliga) in
terms of shooting tendencies and efficiency. We found players in higher levels to
be more risky and aim for top corners even though the possibility of missing the
target is higher there. They are also more predictable in terms of where they
shoot from. Goalkeepers seem to get better at saving shots at body level but
have a harder time with shots to bottom corners as they age. We also found out
that distance from goal distributions are significantly different between the four
leagues.

In addition to statistical analysis, we designed, trained and tested Expected
Goals models to examine their weights. They achieved very similar performances
to wyscout's Expected Goals model.

A   Box plots of significantly different distributions

Here you can find the box plots for distributions we've encountered that, according to ANOVA, significantly differ ($p_{value} < 0.05$) between the four leagues.

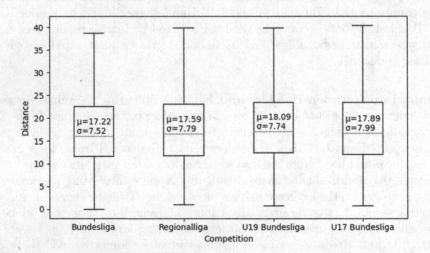

Fig. 4. Distance to goal distributions in different leagues

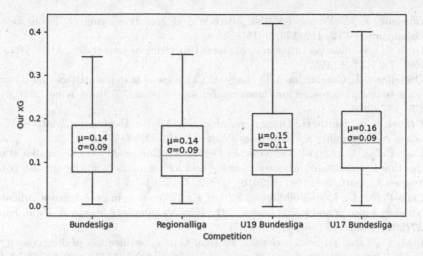

Fig. 5. Our xg score distributions for headers in different leagues

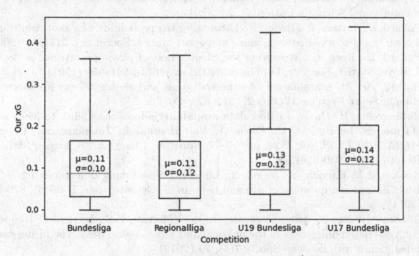

Fig. 6. Our xg score distributions for kicks in different leagues

References

1. StatsBomb   xG.   https://statsbomb.com/articles/soccer/statsbomb-release-expected-goals-with-shot-impact-height/
2. Wyscout shot definintions & parameters. https://dataglossary.wyscout.com/shot/
3. Armatas, V., Yiannakos, A., Papadopoulou, S., Skoufas, D.: Evaluation of goals scored in top ranking soccer matches: Greek Superleague 2006–07. Serbian J. Sports Sci. **3**(1), 39–43 (2009)
4. Benítez-Sillero, J.D.D., Martínez-Aranda, L.M., Sanz-Matesanz, M., Domínguez-Escribano, M.: determining factors of psychological performance and differences among age categories in youth football players. Sustainability **13**(14), 7713 (2021)

5. Bonsang, E., Dohmen, T.: Risk attitude and cognitive aging. J. Econ. Behav. Organization **112**, 112–126 (2015)
6. Brier, G.: Verification of forecast expressed in terms of probability. Mon. Weather Rev. **78**(1), 1–3 (1950)
7. Castellano, J., Casamichana, D., Lago, C.: The use of match statistics that discriminate between successful and unsuccessful soccer teams. J. Hum. Kinet. **31**(2012), 137–147 (2012)
8. Draper, N.R., Smith, H.: Dummy variables. In: Applied Regression Analysis. Wiley Series in Probability and Statistics, Wiley, 1 edn. (1998)
9. Lago-Peñas, C., Lago-Ballesteros, J., Dellal, A., Gómez, M.: Game-related statistics that discriminated winning, drawing and losing teams from the Spanish soccer league. J. Sports Sci. Med. **9**(2010), 288–293 (2010)
10. Lago-Peñas, C., Lago-Ballesteros, J., Rey, E.: Differences in performance indicators between winning and losing teams in the UEFA champions league. J. Hum. Kinet. **27**(2011), 135–146 (2011)
11. Link, D., Lang, S., Seidenschwarz, P.: Real time quantification of dangerousity in football using spatiotemporal tracking data. PLoS ONE **11**(12), e0168768 (2016)
12. Pappalardo, L., et al.: A public data set of spatio-temporal match events in soccer competitions. Scientific Data **6**(1), 236 (2019)
13. Pollard, R., Ensum, J., Taylor, S.: Estimating the probability of a shot resulting in a goal: the effects of distance, angle and space. Int. J. Soccer Sci. **2**(1), 15 (2004)
14. Pollard, R., Reep, C.: Measuring the effectiveness of playing strategies at soccer. J. Royal Statist. Soc. Ser. D (The Statistician) **46**(4), 541–550 (1997)
15. Rathke, A.: An examination of expected goals and shot efficiency in soccer. J. Human Sport Exercise **12**(Proc2), 514–529 (2017)
16. Robberechts, P., Davis, J.: How data availability affects the ability to learn good xG models. In: Brefeld, U., Davis, J., Van Haaren, J., Zimmermann, A. (eds.) MLSA 2020. CCIS, vol. 1324, pp. 17–27. Springer, Cham (2020). https://doi.org/10.1007/978-3-030-64912-8_2
17. Rolison, J.J., Hanoch, Y., Wood, S., Liu, P.J.: Risk-taking differences across the adult life span: a question of age and domain. J. Gerontol. Ser. B **69**(6), 870–880 (2014)
18. Rábano-Muñoz, A., Asian-Clemente, J., de Villarreal, E.S., Nayler, J., Requena, B.: Age-related differences in the physical and physiological demands during small-sided games with floaters. Sports **7**(4), 79 (2019)
19. Tippett, J.: The expected goals philosophy: a game-changing way of analysing football. Independently Published (2019)
20. Trninić, V., Trninić, M., Penezić, Z.: Personality differences between the players regarding the type of sport and age. Acta Kinesiologica **10**(2), 69–74 (2016)
21. Vars, F.E.: Missing well: optimal targeting of soccer shots. Chance **22**(4), 21–28 (2009)
22. Witmore, J.: The analyst - what are expected goals? (2019). https://theanalyst.com/eu/2021/07/what-are-expected-goals-xg/
23. Witmore, J.: Evolving Expected Goals (xG) (2022). https://theanalyst.com/eu/2022/03/evolving-expected-goals-xg/
24. Worville, T.: What age do players in different positions peak? (2021). https://theathletic.com/2935360/2021/11/15/what-age-do-players-in-different-positions-peak/

Analyzing Passing Sequences for the Prediction of Goal-Scoring Opportunities

Conor McCarthy[1]([✉]) [iD], Panagiotis Tampakis[1] [iD], Marco Chiarandini[1] [iD],
Morten Bredsgaard Randers[2,3] [iD], Stefan Jänicke[1] [iD], and Arthur Zimek[1] [iD]

[1] Department of Mathematics and Computer Science, University of Southern
Denmark, Odense, Denmark
conor099@hotmail.com, {ptampakis,marco,stjaenicke,zimek}@imada.sdu.dk
[2] Department of Sports Science and Clinical Biomechanics, University of Southern
Denmark, Odense, Denmark
mranders@health.sdu.dk
[3] School of Sport Sciences, Faculty of Health Sciences, UiT The Arctic University
of Norway, Tromsø, Norway

Abstract. Over the last years, more and more sport related data are
being collected, stored, and analyzed to give valuable insights. Football
is no exception to this trend. An important way of identifying a team's
"style" of play is through analyzing passing sequences. However, passing sequences either concentrate on the specific players involved or the
structure of passes and ignore where these sequences took place. In this
paper, we focus on identifying frequent passing zone subsequences that
lead to created or conceded goal scoring opportunities. We partition the
pitch into a set of disjoint zones and apply sequential pattern mining.
Our experimental study on the 2020/21 Danish Superliga season shows
that our method is able to predict goal scoring opportunities better than
random subsequences that occurred, in median, 99.5% of the cases.

1 Introduction

During the last years, the analysis of data from professional football has attracted
a lot of attention. A hot topic in the football world is a team's "style" of play.
There are numerous styles that teams commonly have, including: possession,
high pressing, and direct play. How teams try to score or concede goals is a
defining factor in their style of play, as, ultimately, the goal of a game of football
is to try to score more goals than the other team. Towards this direction, there
have been some efforts for analysing offensive and defensive strategies [3,13,18].
However, most of them focus on plain statistical analysis, which could ignore
hidden patterns that might exist in the data and that could be identified by
more knowledge discovery techniques on tracking data, such as clustering [12,17]
and outlier detection [15,21]. A popular way of analysing the style of play of
a team is through its passing sequences [1,6], where a passing network gets

U. Brefeld et al. (Eds.): MLSA 2022, CCIS 1783, pp. 27–40, 2023.
https://doi.org/10.1007/978-3-031-27527-2_3

constructed, which is a graph where the nodes represent the players and the edges the passes between players. Nevertheless, this approach concentrates on the identity of the players involved in passing sequences rather than on roles [14] or on the structure of the passes risks to capture only a partial representation of a team's play style. Flow motifs [9], which are sequences of three consecutive, uninterrupted passes involving a maximum of four distinct players, where labels represent distinct players without identity, try to overcome this limitation by focusing on the structure of a passing sequence. To exemplify, let us consider a passing sequence 2–4–2–4, where player 2 passes to player 4, player 4 passes back to player 2 and player 2 back to player 4. The corresponding flow motif is ABAB. Then, 4–2–4–5 (the next consecutive 3 passes) turns into ABAC. On the other hand, flow motifs disregard the area on the pitch where the passing sequence took place, which might give us significant insight.

Motivated by these previous works, we also focus on identifying frequent passing sequences that lead to created or conceded goal scoring opportunities. However, rather than considering individual players we consider areas on the pitch from where the passes occur. To achieve this, we partition the pitch into a set of disjoint zones and utilize these zones to discover *frequent zone subsequences* that lead to a created or conceded goal scoring opportunity, as illustrated in Fig. 1. The rest of the paper is organized as follows, in Sect. 2 we formally define the problem, in Sect. 3 we provide details about our methodology and in Sect. 4 we present the findings of our study. Finally, in Sect. 6 we conclude and discuss about future directions of our work.

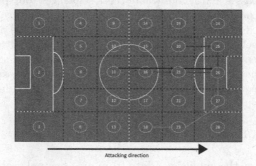

Fig. 1. Visualisation of Brøndby IF's top 3 most frequent zone subsequences that lead to a goal-scoring opportunities.

2   Problem Definition

Definition 1 *(Tracking Data). The tracking data T of a game consist of a sequence of semantically enriched timestamped locations $\langle p_1, p_2, \ldots, p_N \rangle$, where N is the number of samples. Each data point p_i, $i \in [1, N]$ consists of a tuple*

$p_i = (x_i, y_i, z_i, t_i, tp_i)$, where x_i, y_i, z_i designate the position of the ball in the pitch, t_i the timestamp, and tp_i the team in possession of the ball at time t_i.

Definition 2 *(Tracking Subsequence).* A tracking subsequence $T_{i,j}$, $i < j$, is a subsequence $\langle p_i, \dots, p_j \rangle$ of T that contains all semantically enriched timestamped locations of the ball between t_i and t_j.

Definition 3 *(Event Data).* Each game consists of a set of events $E = \{e_1, e_2, \dots, e_M\}$. Each event e_j for $j \in [1, M]$ consists of a tuple $e_j = (x_j, y_j, t_j, et_j)$, where x_j, y_j denote the x and y coordinates, t_j the timestamp, and $et_j \in ET$ the event type.

The set of event types ET contains different kinds of events, such as pass, foul or interception. These events can be grouped into two large groups, i.e., events that change the possession of the ball, called CPE, e.g., an interception or a successful tackle, and events that do not change the possession, called $nCPE$. Clearly, $CPE \cap nCPE = \emptyset$. Thus $ET = CPE \cup nCPE$. We assume that the tracking and event data have been aligned (see later for details), that is, the timestamp and coordinates of every event $e_j \in E$ have been matched with exactly one data point from the tracking data T. We break the large sequence of tracking and event data that correspond to an entire game into smaller portions, each portion corresponding to a ball possession by a team, by utilizing CPE.

Definition 4 *(Possession Subsequences).* The collection of ball possessions for a specific team is denoted by $PS = \{ps_1, ps_2, \dots, ps_Q\}$. Each ps_k corresponds to a tracking subsequence T_{i_k, j_k} of T with $et_{i_k}, et_{j_k} \in CPE$ and $et_l \in nCPE$ for all $l \in [i_k + 1, j_k - 1]$.

We are interested not in all possessions but only in those leading to a goal scoring opportunity. Such events are possession for a team ending with them scoring a goal, winning a penalty, or taking a shot on goal that did not end in a goal.

Definition 5 *(Goal Scoring Opportunity Subsequences).* The collection of ball possessions that lead to a goal scoring opportunity is denoted by $GSO = \{gso_1, gso_2, \dots, gso_R\}$. GSO is a subset of PS, $GSO \subseteq PS$, and for each gso_k, $k \in [1, R], R < Q$, it is $et_{j_k} \in \{Goal, Penalty, ShotOnGoal\}$.

Several knowledge extraction techniques, such as sequential pattern mining, would not benefit by the exact position of the ball at a specific timestamp. For this reason, we decided to ignore the temporal dimension and consider only the sequence of ball positions. Furthermore, we chose to abstract the spatial dimension at a higher level by partitioning the pitch in a set of zones.

Definition 6 *(Pitch Partitioning).* A pitch can be considered to consist of a set of zones $P = \{z_1, z_2, \dots, z_S\}$, where each $z_i \in P$ is a rectangle defined by $(zid_i, lx_i, ly_i, hx_i, hy_i)$, with zid_i being the zone identifiers and lx_i, ly_i and hx_i, hy_i being the coordinates of the lower and higher corners, respectively. It holds that $\cap_{i \in [1,S]} z_i = \emptyset$ and $\cup_{i \in [1,S]} z_i$ covers the whole pitch.

Now, by spatially overlapping each $ps_k \in gso_m \in GSO$ with P, we can remove the exact spatial position and replace it with the zone id. Furthermore, we can remove the exact timestamp and keep only the sequence of zones. Finally, we can eliminate successive duplicate zone appearances. By doing so, we result in having zone sequences instead of opportunity possessions.

Definition 7 *(Goal Scoring Opportunity Zone Sequence). Formally, a zone sequence $zs \in ZS$ is defined as $zs = \{zid_1, zid_2, \ldots, zid_{|zs|}\}$, where $zid_i \neq zid_j \forall i, j \in [1, |zs|]$. It is obvious that $\forall gso_m \in GSO$ we get a $zs_m \in ZS$.*

Each goal scoring opportunity zone sequence $zs \in ZS$ is a string of identifiers (e.g., integer numbers) for which we distinguish substrings and subsequences.

Definition 8 *(Zone Substring). A zone substring $zs_{i,j}$ of $zs = \langle zid_1, zid_2, \ldots, zid_\ell \rangle$ is defined as $\langle zid_i, zid_{i+1}, \ldots, zid_j \rangle$, that is, the set of consecutive elements from zs between position $i \geq 1$ and position $j \leq \ell$, where $i \leq j$.*

Definition 9 *(Zone Subsequence). A zone subsequence zs' consists of $\langle zs_{i,j}, zs_{k,l}, \ldots zs_{m,n} \rangle$, with $i \leq j < k \leq l < m \leq n$, can be defined as a set of zone substrings contained in zs.*

Definition 10 *(Support). For a collection of zone sequences of goal scoring opportunities, $ZS = \{zs_1, zs_2, \ldots, zs_R\}$, the support of a zone subsequence zs' is defined as $\mathrm{support}(zs', ZS) = |\{zs \in ZS \mid zs' \text{ is a subsequence of } zs\}|/R$.*

We can now formalize our problem as follows.

Definition 11 *(Frequent Zone Subsequence Discovery). Given a set T of tracking data, a set E of event data, a pitch partitioning P and a minimum support threshold τ, our task is to retrieve from the collection of zone sequences of goal scoring opportunities, ZS, the set ZS^* of zones subsequences with support above the threshold τ, that is, to determine $ZS^* = \{zs' \mid \exists zs \in ZS, zs' \text{ is subsequence of } zs \wedge \mathrm{support}(zs', ZS) \geq \tau\}$.*

3   Methodology

In Fig. 2 we summarize the methodology that we used to tackle the problem defined in Sect. 2. Initially, we perform a preprocessing step to align the event and tracking data. Subsequently, we utilize the enriched tracking data to extract the goal scoring opportunity subsequences GSO. The pitch partitioning step can be performed either successively or in parallel with the GSO extraction step, depending on whether the partitioning is data-driven or not. Next, the $GSOs$ are compressed into Zone Sequences. Finally, the Frequent Zone Subsequences are discovered by preforming Sequential Pattern Mining on the Zone Sequences.

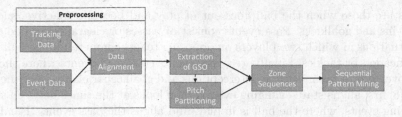

Fig. 2. Overview of the methodology.

3.1 Tracking Data

The actual tracking data utilized in this paper were provided by ChyronHego, which used the TRACAB Image Tracking System [2] to track the location of players, referees, and the ball (at a frequency 25 Hz) during matches for the Danish Superliga during the 2020/21 season. In our case we utilized only the location of the ball. Each tuple of the dataset consists of (1) x, (2) y, (3) z, (4) the speed, (5) the team in possession and (6) the ball status (ball in play or not). For our analysis, we used only the attributes that are defined in Definition 1 and the tuples where the ball is in play.

3.2 Event Data

The event data for each match are created by the company Opta. It should be noted that the Opta event data are not automated but created manually by people who are assigned to watch a game live. Each tuple of the event data consisting of (1) an id, (2) a $type\_id$, (3) $period\_id$ (1st or 2nd half), (4) t (the timestamp), (5) x, (6) y (7) $player\_id$, (8) $team\_id$, (9) $outcome$, and (10) $qualifiers$ (additional detail about an event). At this point, we should mention that every shot taken throughout a match has a qualifier that states the expected goal value (xG) for that shot. The expected goal value, xG, is a measure of the quality of a scoring opportunity based on the probability of a shot being performed from a particular position during a particular passage of play. The model used by Opta takes many different variables into account when predicting this probability of a shot leading to a goal [4]. It uses logistic regression with the response variable being whether a shot resulted in a goal or not. From these values, it is possible to get a decent idea as to how likely a shooting opportunity is to end in a goal.

3.3 Data Alignment

As already mentioned, the event data were manually annotated and for this reason there might exist inconsistencies between the event data and the tracking data. For the analysis of these data, it was necessary to align these two datasets and in order to achieve this we utilized the work done by Kuzmicki [8], where the events are divided into four categories (sub-problems): (1) state-changing events, (2) pass events, (3) duels, and (4) recovery events. The state-changing events are those when the ball goes out of play and becomes inactive, such as throw-ins and goalkicks. Pass events consist of passes or clearances, while duels are situations in which two players on opposing teams compete for the ball such as in headers or tackles. Finally, recovery events consist of events where the ball is recovered by a team, such as interceptions and goalkeeper claims. The method from [8] first aligns state-changing events, then looks at the times between state-changing events, where the ball is in play, and aligns the pass events. Finally, it aligns duels and then recovery events.

To align the state-changing events, the times in the tracking data when the status of the ball goes from alive to dead were considered and aligned with the corresponding state-changing events that were within two seconds, according to the timestamps in the event data. The event-types that are aligned in this manner are, throw-ins and goalkicks (outs), corners, offsides, fouls, goals, game/half starting, and game/half ending. Once the state-changing events are aligned, to align the passes, two sequences were extracted between every state-changing event when the ball is in play, one from the tracking and one from the event. From the event data, the sequence of pass performers between the state-changing events were looked at, and from the tracking data, the sequence of 'ball possessors' were extracted, where a 'ball possessor' is a person that is within 1.5 m of the ball during any frame between the two state-changing events, as defined by Kuzmicki. These two sequences are then aligned using the Needleman-Wunsch algorithm [10]. The event-types that are aligned in this manner are, passes, offside passes, clearances, shot misses, shots that hit the post, saves by goalkeepers, and ball touches. Some of these events obviously aren't actually passes, but they can be aligned using the same principle. After the state-changing events and passes have been aligned, the events where duels occur are aligned. For duel events, there are two events in the event data, one for each player involved. To align these events, the distances between both players and the ball are calculated, and the frame where the minimum sum of these distances occurs is aligned with the two events. Finally, for the alignment of the recovery events, the time-frame between events where these events can occur, is much smaller, due to the other events already previously being aligned. The recovery events are aligned by looking at these timeframes, and aligning the instant that the ball comes within 1.5 m of the player doing the event. Some events get misaligned in the process of the sequence alignment, this can happen for a number of reasons, the event data assigned an event to the wrong player, an event was recorded in the event data that never occurred, or an event occurred but was never recorded in the event data. Kuzmicki added an enrichment process to the alignment where he corrected some of the mismatched events and also added other event-types. The correction of some of the events is based on the assumption that the tracking data is more accurate than the event data, as the tracking is automated and the event is manual.

3.4   Extraction of Goal Scoring Opportunities

To extract the goal scoring opportunities we follow a slightly different approach than the one defined in Definition 5. More specifically, we rely on a previous work [5]. Accordingly, an expected goal value, xG, greater than or equal to 0.33 constitutes a "big chance" for a team. Hence, we considered as goal scoring opportunities only sequences with xG above this threshold.

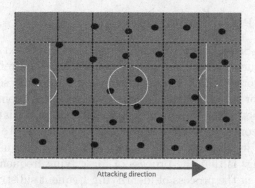

Fig. 3. Selected pitch partitioning, overlapped with the centroids produced by k-means.

Goals that occur from set pieces, i.e., corners, free kicks, do not produce very interesting sequences, as they contain either just a cross into the box or a shot, and the team is not really in physical control of the ball when it is in the air after being crossed. Therefore, even if it is estimated that approximately 30–40% of all goals in professional football are from set pieces [20], nevertheless, we decided to exclude all set pieces from our analysis.

3.5   Pitch Partitioning

Once the goal-scoring opportunity sequences have been extracted, the next step is to see what areas of the pitch the ball passes through during these sequences. Different ways of partitioning the pitch have been proposed [7,19] and any of them could be used here. For this work, we decided to use a similar method to the one proposed in [16] because it includes the "half spaces" that are of particular interest to football coaches. However, we changed the defensive third into 3 zones instead of 5, as there are substantially fewer passes in these areas, thus, yielding 28 instead of 30 zones. We also decided to flip the numbers so that a team's defensive areas are the lower numbers and attacking areas are the higher, always. The selected pitch partitioning can be seen in Fig. 3. However, other disjoint pitch partitioning solutions can be applied seamlessly, since this is orthogonal to our problem.

An alternative approach was to use the data in the goal-scoring opportunity sequences to infer the areas of the pitch from where passes are most frequently performed. We pooled the coordinates of every pass from all teams' goal-scoring opportunity sequences to get a generalised idea of all pass locations. We actually utilized this approach to verify the selected partitioning by applying the k-means clustering method (with $k = 28$). The results illustrated in Fig. 3 showed that, even though the partitioning selected above and the zones produced by the k-means approach are not perfectly aligned, they have a striking similarity, since most of the zones only contain one cluster centroid.

3.6   Sequential Pattern Mining

Finally, we apply a Sequential Pattern Mining algorithm to extract the most Frequent Zone Subsequences. For this purpose, we utilized the PrefixSpan sequential pattern mining algorithm [11]. The algorithm is a depth first search (DFS) algorithm that mines for *subsequences* instead of *substrings*. As defined in Sect. 2, the actual difference between subsequences and substrings is that a substring is a set of consecutive zones, while a subsequence is a set similar to a substring, with the difference that it allows for zone "gaps". The reason for using subsequences instead of substrings is that the process of identifying frequent subsequences is less constrained than the process of identifying frequent substrings, hence it will produce more frequent patterns to analyse, yielding more robust results.

4   Experimental Study

Our experimental assessment is as follows. Initially, we apply our methodology and extract the Frequent Zone Subsequences, both for created and conceded goal scoring opportunities. Then, we calculate an accuracy measure to assess how accurate the sequential patterns found are for predicting goal-scoring opportunities for each team. Finally, this accuracy measure is compared to frequently occurring zone subsequences that are randomly extracted from the dataset. The length of these subsequences is equal to the length of the discovered frequent zone subsequences that lead to a goal scoring opportunity. These subsequences represent those that are commonly found during a match, and hence comparing their accuracy against the one of the discovered Frequent Zone Subsequences unveils how unlikely it is for a random subsequence to achieve better accuracy than the discovered Frequent Zone Subsequences.

We split the data into a training set and a test set. Thus, for each team's zone sequences of goal-scoring opportunities throughout the whole season, a training set ZS_{train} is extracted consisting of 70% of these sequences. In this training set, the frequent zone subsequences ZS^* are extracted for each team. The remaining 30% are then used as the test set ZS_{test}, which is used to test if the frequent zone subsequences ZS^* from the training set ZS_{train} actually appear in the unseen test set zone sequences as goal-scoring opportunities.

We measure the accuracy of ZS^* as the percentage of the number of sequences from ZS_{test} that contain at least one sequence from ZS^* as subsequence, over the total number of sequences in the test set. More formally, for a team the accuracy of its ZS^* can be defined as

$$\text{Accuracy} = \frac{|\{zs \in ZS_{\text{test}} \mid \exists\, \widehat{zs} \in ZS^*, \widehat{zs} \text{ is subsequence of } zs\}|}{|ZS_{\text{test}}|}. \quad (1)$$

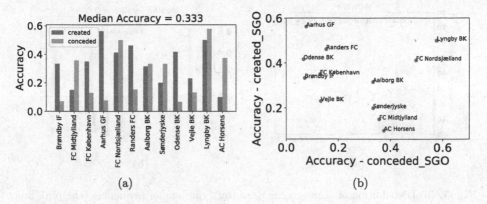

(a)   (b)

Fig. 4. Accuracy of created vs conceded GSO (a) bar chart and (b) scatter plot.

The accuracy results for both created and conceded GSOs are depicted in Fig. 4. The x-axis of Fig. 4(a) shows the teams sorted from left to right according to their final ranking, while the y-axis reports the accuracy for both created and conceded goals. The median overall accuracy is 0.333, but it is hard to interpret if this is a "good" accuracy.

Figure 4(b) illustrates how each team performs in terms of accuracy, both for created and conceded GSOs. For example, we can clearly see that Lyngby is the dominant team in terms of conceded GSO accuracy and in terms of created GSO accuracy. This can be interpreted as an indication that this specific team plays in a predictable way both offensively and defensively, which led to poor performance as the final ranking of this team was second to last. On the other hand, Vejle, which seems to be one of the most unpredictable teams finished third from the bottom. A possible explanation to these opposite results for the two teams might be the different number of sequences that led to a GSO in the test set, which affects the denominator of Eq. 1.

To deal with this, we tried to measure how much "better", in terms of accuracy, ZS^* performs in the test set, in comparison to a set of random subsequences ZS^* drawn from each team's top 500 most frequent zone subsequences that occurred throughout the season extracted from all possession sequences PS (hence, irrespective of whether they ended in a GSO). We construct the empirical distribution of the accuracy of 100 random subsequences ZS^* as follows. For each team, we repeat 100 times the sampling of a set of subsequences ZS^* of the same size as ZS^* from the 500 subsequences. Let B be the set of the sampled ZS^*. Then, for each random sample $ZS^* \in B$, the accuracy on the test set ZS_{test} is calculated. From these 100 accuracy values we derive the empirical distribution as illustrated in Fig. 5. The likelihood of the accuracy of ZS^* is then the fraction of the samples from B that have a lower accuracy. A value of the likelihood close to zero indicates that the frequent zone subsequence is exceptional.

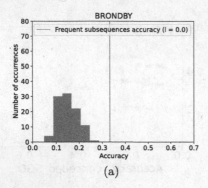
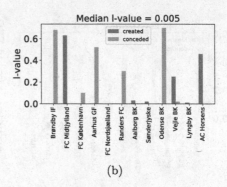

(a)   (b)

Fig. 5. (a) Distribution of accuracy for Brondby's random subsequences (the pink line is the accuracy of ZS^*) and (b) likelihood of the accuracy of ZS^*.

Figure 5(a), shows the distribution of the accuracy of random sequences along with the accuracy achieved (pink line) by the discovered frequent zone subsequences that lead to a GSO. Figure 5(b), depicts the likelihood value for each team both for created and conceded GSOs. We can see that most of the teams achieve a likelihood value close to zero. In addition, we can observe that the median likelihood value is $0.005 = 0.5\%$, indicating that the frequent zone subsequences from the proposed methodology lead to exceptionally high accuracy. Regarding Lyngby and Vejle, we can observe that Lyngby's extracted frequent zone subsequences are significant, since it has an l-value close to zero both for conceded and created opportunities. On the other hand, Vejle has a high value for created opportunities, which means that the extracted frequent zone subsequences for created opportunities are not so "trustworthy" and we should not base our analysis on them.

5   Style of Play for the Top-2 Teams

In this section we focus on the top-2 teams individually and use their frequent zonal subsequences from goal-scoring opportunity sequences, as well as their frequent pass locations during these sequences, to get an idea as to what "style" of play each team has.

The winners of the league during the Danish Superliga 2020/21 season were Brøndby IF (BIF). Over the course of the season, they created the most goal-scoring opportunities, 67, and they conceded the second-least, 43, for teams in

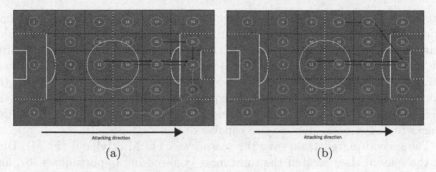

Fig. 6. Top 3 most frequent zone subsequences that lead to a goal-scoring opportunities of (a) Brøndby IF and (b) Midtjylland.

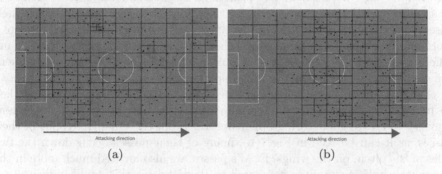

Fig. 7. Quadtree on passes made by (a) Brøndby IF and (b) Midtjylland.

the Championship round. From the analysis of the significance of their frequent subsequences on these chances, presented in the previous section, it was seen that their observed accuracy was significantly better than their random accuracies for their created opportunities, but not for their conceded opportunities.

This suggests that the top-3 frequent subsequences from created goal-scoring opportunities found for BIF over the course of the season were highly significant in explaining how they created opportunities. The top 3 frequent subsequences found in all these goal-scoring opportunity sequences can be seen in Fig. 6(a). It should be noted that because the sequences are subsequences, which allow gaps, the visualisation does not necessarily perfectly show the exact path for each subsequence. In Fig. 7(a), the areas where most passes occurred during goal-scoring opportunities are visualised, using the Quadtrees method of splitting the pitch to show the most dense areas.

Combining the two figures showing the frequent subsequences and the pass densities, it appears that BIF tend to create a lot of their opportunities down the middle of the pitch with passes starting from their own half. They also appear to make a lot of use of the "half-spaces" 25 and 27, with a lot of passes occurring in both. Interestingly, there are 2 frequent subsequences attacking down the right side of the pitch, but not an abundance of passes actually occur here, perhaps suggesting that BIF play passes through this part of the pitch a lot, but don't actually make that many passes in them. The high density of passes just inside their own half on the right also indicate this. Indeed, BIF had a lot of shots after fast breaks, which would explain the sequences from the right, which indicate that BIF counterattacked down this side a lot during the season. Overall, the majority of BIF's passes during the sequences occur in their own half of the pitch, which could suggest that they are a patient team that enjoy building attacks from the back, but are also capable of quick counterattacks.

The second-placed team over the season was FC Midtjylland (FCM). During the season, they created the third most goal-scoring opportunities, 62, and they conceded the joint second-least, 43, for teams in the Championship round. Analysing the significance of FCM's frequent subsequences from goal-scoring opportunity sequences, their subsequences for created chances were not found to be significant, but the subsequences for their conceded were. The fact that their observed accuracy was not found to be significant could indicate that FCM are a more unpredictable team than others when creating chances, as they have many different areas of the pitch that they look to attack from. FCM's top 3 frequent zonal subsequences from goal-scoring opportunities can be seen in Fig. 6(b).

As FCM's frequent subsequences were not found to be significant to how they create chances, there should be less emphasis on looking at these to define how they try to create goal-scoring opportunities. From the Quadtrees split of their passes, as it can be seen in Fig. 7(b), many of their passes occur down the two sides of the pitch, on the wings. FCM's passes are also located much more in the opponent's half of the pitch compared to Brøndby IF, this could indicate that FCM are a much higher pressing team, gaining success from creating chances when winning the ball in the opponent's half. Overall, FCM seem to be a team that have a lot of variation in how they attack, with their frequent subsequences not being significant, and they appear to emphasise intricate passing in the opponent's half of the pitch in order to create chances. Indeed, FCM has a very dynamic attack with players constantly changing positions, and that they tend to dominate matches with a lot of possession and high pressure.

6   Conclusions and Future Work

We focused on identifying frequent passing zone subsequences that lead to created or conceded goal scoring opportunities. We proposed a methodology, consisting of (1) a preprocessing step that aligns event and tracking data, (2) the extraction of goal scoring opportunities, (3) the partitioning of the pitch into a set of zones, (4) the extraction of zone sequences, and (5) the discovery of frequent zone subsequences. The results indicate that our method is able to perform better than random subsequences that occurred, in median, 99.5% of the cases.

For the future, we plan to cross validate the results on different settings of training and test sets, either by using k-fold cross validation, or by using the first round as a training set and trying to predict the second round. Moreover, we plan to perform some sensitivity analysis with respect to the value of xG.

Furthermore, we would like to work on a good methodology of data-driven pitch partitioning. Finally, we plan to use a spatial sequence similarity measure for the calculation of accuracy, instead of the containment presented in Eq. 1.

References

1. Barbosa, A., Ribeiro, P., Dutra, I.: Similarity of football players using passing sequences. In: Brefeld, U., Davis, J., Van Haaren, J., Zimmermann, A. (eds.) MLSA 2021. CCIS, vol. 1571, pp. 51–61. Springer, Cham (2021). https://doi.org/10.1007/978-3-031-02044-5_5
2. ChryonHego: TRACAB optical tracking product information sheet. Technical report, ChryronHego (2019). https://chyronhego.com/wp-content/uploads/2019/01/TRACAB-PI-sheet.pdf
3. Fernandez-Navarro, J., Fradua, L., Zubillaga, A., Ford, P.R., McRobert, A.P.: Attacking and defensive styles of play in soccer: analysis of Spanish and English elite teams. J. Sports Sci. **34**(24), 2195–2204 (2016)
4. Gregory, S.: Expected Goals in Context (2017). https://www.statsperform.com/resource/expected-goals-in-context/
5. Hernanz, J.: How good is Driblab's Expected Goals (xG) model? (2021). https://www.driblab.com/analysis-team/how-good-is-driblabs-expected-goals-xg-model/
6. Hughes, M., Franks, I.: Analysis of passing sequences, shots and goals in soccer. J. Sports Sci. **23**(5), 509–514 (2005)
7. Kim, J., James, N., Parmar, N., Ali, B., Vučković, G.: The attacking process in football: a taxonomy for classifying how teams create goal scoring opportunities using a case study of crystal palace FC. Front. Psychol. **10**, 1–8 (2019)
8. Kuźmicki, P.: Synchronizaton, enrichment and visualizaton of football data. Master's thesis, University of Southern Denmark (SDU) (2020)
9. Malqui, J.L.S., Romero, N.M.L., Garcia, R., Alemdar, H., Comba, J.L.: How do soccer teams coordinate consecutive passes? A visual analytics system for analysing the complexity of passing sequences using soccer flow motifs. Comput. Graph. **84**, 122–133 (2019)
10. Needleman, S.B., Wunsch, C.D.: A general method applicable to the search for similarities in the amino acid sequence of two proteins. J. Mol. Biol. **48**(3), 443–453 (1970)
11. Pei, J., et al.: PrefixSpan: mining sequential patterns efficiently by prefix-projected pattern growth. In: Proceedings 17th International Conference on Data Engineering, pp. 215–224 (2001)
12. Pelekis, N., Tampakis, P., Vodas, M., Panagiotakis, C., Theodoridis, Y.: In-DBMS sampling-based sub-trajectory clustering. In: Proceedings of the 20th International Conference on Extending Database Technology, EDBT 2017, Venice, Italy, 21–24 March 2017, pp. 632–643. OpenProceedings.org (2017)
13. Rahimian, P., Toka, L.: Inferring the strategy of offensive and defensive play in soccer with inverse reinforcement learning. In: Brefeld, U., Davis, J., Van Haaren, J., Zimmermann, A. (eds.) MLSA 2021. CCIS, vol. 1571, pp. 26–38. Springer, Cham (2021). https://doi.org/10.1007/978-3-031-02044-5_3
14. Sattari, A., Johansson, U., Wilderoth, E., Jakupovic, J., Larsson-Green, P.: The interpretable representation of football player roles based on passing/receiving patterns. In: Brefeld, U., Davis, J., Van Haaren, J., Zimmermann, A. (eds.) MLSA 2021. CCIS, vol. 1571, pp. 62–76. Springer, Cham (2021). https://doi.org/10.1007/978-3-031-02044-5_6

15. Schubert, E., Zimek, A., Kriegel, H.: Local outlier detection reconsidered: a generalized view on locality with applications to spatial, video, and network outlier detection. Data Min. Knowl. Discov. **28**(1), 190–237 (2014)
16. Seymour, D.: Tactical theory: using the half-spaces to progress the ball (2020). https://totalfootballanalysis.com/article/tactical-theory-using-half-spaces-progress-ball-tactical-analysis-tactics
17. Tampakis, P., Pelekis, N., Doulkeridis, C., Theodoridis, Y.: Scalable distributed subtrajectory clustering. In: 2019 IEEE International Conference on Big Data (IEEE BigData), Los Angeles, CA, USA, 9–12 December 2019, pp. 950–959. IEEE (2019)
18. Tenga, A., Holme, I., Ronglan, L.T., Bahr, R.: Effect of playing tactics on achieving score-box possessions in a random series of team possessions from Norwegian professional soccer matches. J. Sports Sci. **28**(3), 245–255 (2010)
19. Tianbiao, L., Andreas, H.: Apriori-based diagnostical analysis of passings in the football game. In: 2016 IEEE International Conference on Big Data Analysis (ICBDA), pp. 1–4 (2016)
20. Yiannakos, A., Armatas, V.: Evaluation of the goal scoring patterns in European Championship in Portugal 2004. Int. J. Perform. Anal. Sport **6**, 178–188 (2006)
21. Zimek, A., Filzmoser, P.: There and back again: outlier detection between statistical reasoning and data mining algorithms. WIREs Data Mining Knowl. Discov. **8**(6) (2018). https://doi.org/10.1002/widm.1280

Let's Penetrate the Defense: A Machine Learning Model for Prediction and Valuation of Penetrative Passes

Pegah Rahimian[1]([✉]), Dayana Grayce da Silva Guerra Gomes[1],
Fanni Berkovics[1], and Laszlo Toka[1,2]

[1] Budapest University of Technology and Economics, Budapest, Hungary
{pegah.rahimian,gomes.dayanagrayce,fanni.berkovics}@edu.bme.hu,
toka.laszlo@vik.bme.hu
[2] MTA-BME Information Systems Research Group, Budapest, Hungary

Abstract. Moving forward and penetrating the defensive zones is crucial for goal scoring in soccer games, yet it involves risky tactics. We propose a novel metric called Expected Value of Potential Penetrative Pass, which measures the likelihood of a potential penetrative pass creating scoring/conceding situations. We show how such a pass value accounting for the effects of crossing defense lines can be decomposed into elementary components. Using the UEFA EURO 2020 spatiotemporal dataset, we train several conventional machine learning and deep learning models to estimate these expected values for all potential penetrative pass situations in the dataset. For the best five and worst five teams in the dataset, we provide a trade-off between the ability to perform penetrative passes, and the expected value of goals those create. Finally, we show the impact of different field sections as the starting location of the penetrative pass to be performed and to create goal scoring situations.

Keywords: Soccer analytics · Deep learning · Penetrative pass

1 Introduction

Soccer is one of the most popular sports in the world. Similar to any other team sport, the interaction between players, passes in particular, are crucial. Passes are the most frequent actions of the soccer games usually reaching around 800 per game [5]. Thus, measuring the pass impact and capability of the players and teams in terms of successful and valuable passes has gained paramount attention among researchers and sports analyzers. Although media focus on metrics such as the number of passes and their success ratio, and the industry cares more about metrics related to scoring opportunities such as key passes, sports data scientists have combined long- and short-term objectives and introduced novel metrics that consider the effect of short term rewards (e.g., a short successful pass in midfield) in long term objectives (e.g., open valuable space somewhere else on the pitch and create scoring chances) [3–5,8,9,11]. However, most of

U. Brefeld et al. (Eds.): MLSA 2022, CCIS 1783, pp. 41–52, 2023.
https://doi.org/10.1007/978-3-031-27527-2_4

these works consider a generic pass or differentiate passes according to their length (e.g., short passes or long balls). On the other hand, Michalczyk in a Stats Perform blog post discusses the effect of line-breaking passes in creating chances[1]. In order to measure the teams' and players' capability of performing penetrative passes, Sotudeh introduces a metric called Potential Penetrative Passes (P3) that measures how they completed the penetrative passes compared to the number of times they had the potential to do so [13]. In this work, we also take into consideration that players need to move forward to create chances and score goals. Furthermore, we concentrate on the penetrative feature of the passes and introduce a decoupled novel metric called Expected Value of Potential Penetrative Pass (xPPP) to measure the likelihood of a potential penetrative pass creating scoring/conceding situations. By analyzing the StatsBomb360 datasets for UEFA EURO 2020, we rank teams according to their performance in penetrative pass completions and the expected value they can create by doing so. We also show the impact of different field sections on their performance.

2　Related Work

Penetrative pass refers to a pass that breaks through the opposition's defensive zone(s). However, it is not straightforward to detect dynamic defensive zone(s) in each situation due to the complex nature of a soccer game. To this end, several studies propose different clustering algorithms for opponent players. Spectral clustering is used by Fernandez et al. [5] to the mean of opponent positions to detect dynamic lines of their formations, and Rahimian et al. [10] to the opponents' locations and velocities to detect pressure on the ball holder. Michalczyk [1] in his Stats Perform blog post proposes Jenks natural breaks optimization with three clusters on outfield players. A role-based approach has been suggested in [2,9] which finds the formation structure and captures if a pass is attempting to break the line of defenders. Our definition of penetrative passes in this work is the most similar to the definition by Sotudeh [13] as when a player is in a passing situation and there is at least a teammate to receive the ball inside a defensive zone (i.e., a polygon created by the opponent players in front of him (c.f. Figure 1)). However, his work does not provide any pass impact model and simply measures the players' and teams' ability to complete penetrative passes, given all the potential penetrative pass situations. With regards to the pass impact, several action valuation models have been proposed (e.g., [3,5,6,9,12]). In this work, we investigate the teams' abilities accounting for their performance in completing penetrative passes, and the expected value they can create by doing so.

3　Penetrative Pass Prediction and Valuation

Penetrating the defense is a key tactic in invasion games. When a penetrative pass gets through an opponent's defensive zone, it removes the players it has

---

[1] https://bit.ly/39uQe6Q.

passed by and gets the player in possession of the ball closer to the goal. However, such passes have their own risks and rewards. A successful penetrative pass can lead the player in possession of the ball closer to scoring a goal, and an unsuccessful one might lead to a possession loss. The main objective of the present work is to develop a decoupled metric that measures the expected penetrative value of a pass (i.e., the likelihood of a potential penetrative pass to create goal opportunities). For this aim, in this section, we first describe the dataset and elaborate on our designed machine learning setups to predict the penetrative passes and measure their impact on goal scoring/conceding. We then introduce our proposed metrics to measure players' and teams' performance in terms of penetrative pass completion and valuation.

3.1 Dataset and Preprocessing

StatsBomb events and StatsBomb360 events datasets[2] for UEFA EURO 2020 were obtained using the statsbombpy API[3]. Both datasets were fetched and then merged. The StatsBomb events dataset contains 110 columns detailing aspects of each event, and the StatsBomb360 events dataset contains 7 columns depicting the position of each player caught in the frame of the action for each event in the visible area. The datasets included all matches played by 24 teams participating in UEFA EURO 2020.

3.2 Potential Penetrative Pass Situation

As the first step, we follow the definition of a potential penetrative pass according to [13], as when a player is in a passing situation and there is at least a teammate to receive the ball inside a defensive zone (i.e., a convex hull created by the opponent players in front of him (c.f. Fig. 1)). For constructing these situations from the dataset, we first filtered the synchronized dataset for all "Forward Pass" actions with any outcomes such as being penetrative or not, and being successful or turnover. This is because we are constructing a pre-event situation. Furthermore, we assume that the first one-third and the last one-fourth of the field should be ignored since passes that originated in these areas are not valuable for our analysis. Thus, we consider only the area between 40 and 90 m on the touchline of the field. Now for all filtered passes, we construct a convex hull from all visible opponent players' locations in front of the ball using ConvexHull class from the spatial library of scipy[4]. Next, we check all visible teammate players' locations in the visible area. If there exists at least one teammate player lying in the created convex hull (as the potential receiver), we mark the frame as the potential penetrative pass situation, and non-potential penetrative pass, otherwise. This is done using Delaunay class from spatial library of scipy[5].

---

[2] https://statsbomb.com/articles/soccer/statsbomb-announce-the-release-of-free-statsbomb-360-data-euro-2020-available-now/.

[3] https://github.com/statsbomb/statsbombpy.

[4] https://docs.scipy.org/doc/scipy/reference/generated/scipy.spatial.ConvexHull.html.

[5] https://docs.scipy.org/doc/scipy/reference/generated/scipy.spatial.Delaunay.html.

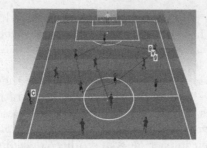

Fig. 1. An example of visible area and a successful penetrative pass

3.3   Penetrative Pass Label Generation

The next step is to check whether or not the potential penetrative pass is completed (i.e., converted into an actual penetrative pass). For this aim, for all potential penetrative pass situations, we check the outcome and receiver of the pass. If the pass was successfully received by one of the teammate players lying in the convex hull, we label the pass as "penetrative". For the rest of the passes including unsuccessful passes, and successful passes received by a teammate player outside of the convex hull, we label them as "non-penetrative".

3.4   Penetrative Pass Decomposed Model

We aim to estimate the likelihood of a potential penetrative pass to create scoring/conceding situations. However, this is a pre-event metric and we still do not know its outcome, i.e., whether it is going to be penetrative or not. Therefore, estimating such a value is not as simple as predicting the probability of goal scoring or conceding within the next preset number of actions. To estimate such a value, we propose a novel decomposed model which takes into consideration different outcomes of a potential penetrative pass, and estimates its likelihood to create scoring/conceding opportunities. To do so, we first introduce the following components:

- **xPP: Expected Value of Penetrative Pass:** Likelihood of an actual penetrative pass to create goal scoring situation;
- **xPC: Expected Penetrative Pass Completion:** Likelihood of a potential penetrative pass completion;
- **xPPP: Expected Value of Potential Penetrative Pass:** Likelihood of a potential penetrative pass to create goal-scoring/conceding situation.

Now we explain how to estimate each component.

xPP: This is a post-event metric, i.e., we know the pass was performed and the outcome was penetrative, and we want to estimate the probability of goal scoring within the next five actions. In order to calculate this metric we have:

$$xPP = \Big(Pr(\text{Penetrative pass} \to goal) \times Value(Goal)\Big) +$$
$$\Big(Pr(\text{Penetrative pass} \to no - goal) \times Value(No - goal)\Big), \tag{1}$$

where $Value(Goal) = 1$, and $Value(No - goal) = 0$. Therefore, we assume that the expected value of a penetrative pass equals to $Pr(\text{Penetrative pass} \to \text{goal})$. We treat estimating this value as a classification model. Since this is a post-event metric, we set the previous 2 actions of the current pass and the pass itself (3 actions in total) as the game state, and predicting goal scoring within the next 5 actions.

xPC: This is a pre-event metric, i.e., we have been given a potential penetrative pass situation, and we are not aware of its outcome. In order to estimate the likelihood of potential penetrative pass completion (i.e., a successful penetrative pass will be completed from a potential situation), we simply train a classification model, by setting the previous three actions of the current potential penetrative pass as the game state, and we set the labels as the outcome of the pass (i.e., penetrative or non-penetrative) like it is elaborated in Sect. 3.3.

xPPP: This is again a pre-event metric, in which we have been given a potential penetrative pass situation without knowing its outcome, and we would like to measure the likelihood of creating goal scoring/conceding within the next 5 actions of the current situation. Estimating this metric depends on the different outcomes of the pass. To this end, we first show how a pass value accounting for the effects of penetration can be decomposed into other components. Thus, we introduce the decoupled xPPP metric in (2):

$$xPPP = \Big(Pr(Penetrative) \times V(Penetrative)\Big) +$$
$$\Big(Pr(Non - Penetrative) \times V(Non - Penetrative)\Big), \tag{2}$$

in which penetrative and non-penetrative passes are complementary events (i.e., $Pr(Penetrative) + Pr(Non - Penetrative) = 1$), and $Pr(Penetrative) = xPC$. V(Penetrative) and V(Non-Penetrative) stand for the value created by performing a pass, assuming to be penetrative or non-penetrative, respectively. To quantify such values, we employ a slightly modified version of the well-known VAEP framework [3] as follows: considering the features of the current pass and the previous two events, we calculate the probability of goal scoring or conceding within the next 10 actions. However, in our setup we set the look-ahead to the next 5 actions as potential penetrative passes are usually in the attacking or established possession phases and might soon result in a goal scoring or conceding. Note that we also differentiate between penetrative and non-penetrative pass actions. Thus, the VAEP framework outputs different values according to the outcome of the actions. Finally, the VAEP framework [3] uses the following Eq. (3) to measure the value of each pass with the respective penetration outcome in our setup:

$$Value(p_i, x|z) = \Delta P_{scores}(p_i, x|z) - \Delta P_{concedes}(p_i, x|z), \tag{3}$$

where p_i stands for a pass action, x is the set of features of each action, and z is the penetration outcome of the pass (i.e., penetrative or non-penetrative), ΔP_{scores} and $\Delta P_{concedes}$ stand for the change in probability of scoring and conceding a goal within next 5 actions after performing a pass, respectively.

4   Experiments and Results

In this section, we first conduct experiments with both conventional machine learning and deep learning models to find the best prediction results for each component of our decomposed model. We then use the prediction results of the winner model for use cases such as teams' performance in terms of penetrative pass completion and value creation.

4.1   Best Performing Prediction Model

In order to get the best result of prediction for each component of our decomposed model, we have trained several machine learning algorithms in the line of VAEP framework [3], setting 3 actions as the game state. For the latter two probabilities, we also included the pass being penetrative or not on top of the VAEP features. The rest of the features are listed in Table 2 for each of the actions in the game state.

The models' parameters were tuned using RandomizedSearchCV, and Pearson correlation was used to select the features (threshold was 0.8), and the highly correlated features were dropped. We chronologically split the dataset into 80% of train, 10% of validation for hyperparameter tuning and model selection, and the remaining 10% as hold-out data for testing. Table 1 shows the evaluation on test set using two classification metrics: ROC AUC, and log-loss (binary cross-entropy).

According to Table 1, the CNN-LSTM model (c.f., Fig. 2) outperforms all other models since it can capture both the spatial (through convolutions layers) and temporal (through recurrent layers) nature of the dataset. For the training process, we used batch size of 64, on Google Colab using Keras sequential models after 10 epochs. Therefore, we continue the analysis of the results estimated by this model.

4.2   Does a Penetrative Pass Affect Goal Scoring or Conceding?

We aim to investigate the effect of penetrative and non-penetrative passes on the probability of goal scoring and conceding within the next 5 actions of the

Table 1. Conventional machine learning and deep learning models evaluation on the test set

Model	xPC		Pr(Scoring)		Pr(Conceding)	
	AUC	Loss	AUC	Loss	AUC	Loss
Logistic regression	0.75	0.45	0.71	0.47	0.66	0.88
XGBoost	0.77	0.41	0.76	0.42	0.71	0.44
Perceptron	0.79	0.40	0.76	0.41	0.74	0.42
CNN	0.81	0.39	0.79	0.40	0.77	0.42
LSTM	0.83	0.35	0.81	0.39	0.80	0.40
LSTM with dropout	0.84	0.35	0.81	0.39	0.81	0.39
CNN-LSTM	0.88	0.32	0.85	0.35	0.84	0.36

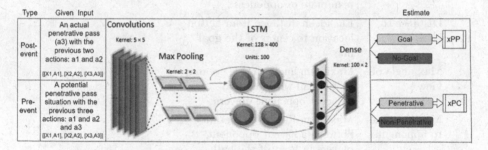

Fig. 2. CNN-LSTM network architecture. Input game states represent both features vector (X), and one-hot vector of actions (A).

current pass. The violin plots in Fig. 3 depict the probability of goal scoring on left, and conceding in right, for all penetrative and non-penetrative passes of the UEFA EURO 2020 dataset. We can see that although the penetrative passes are boosting the probability of goal scoring in comparison to the non-penetrative passes in Fig. 3a (with a median of 0.006 for penetrative and 0.003 for non-penetrative), the non-penetrative passes do not seem to have much effect on boosting the goal conceding probability in Fig. 3b. That is because the non-penetrative passes are not necessarily turnovers and might keep the possession by a side-way pass to a teammate, for instance.

4.3   Teams' Penetrative Performance Analysis

In this section, we evaluate the teams participating in UEFA EURO 2020 in terms of the three introduced metrics: xPP, xPC, and xPPP.

xPP: In order to evaluate how teams are performing in terms of converting a penetrative pass to a goal within the next 5 actions, we sum up their xPP through all their actual penetrative passes. We call this metric as xPP sum, and

Table 2. The game state features list according to their usage for each of the pre-event metrics (e.g., xPC), and post-event metrics (e.g., goal scoring and conceding probabilities from a penetrative pass). We order players using the permutation invariant sorting scheme proposed in [7] in which the ball holder is selected as the anchor in the first position, and the rest of the players are numbered according to their distances to the anchor.

State feature name	Description	Pre-event?	Post-event
Teammates location	(x,y) location of teammates in the visible area	✓	✓
Opponents location	(x,y) location of opponents in the visible area	✓	✓
Team ID	Action is performed by a teammate or opponent?	✓	✓
Distance to goal	Euclidean distance from action location to center of the goal line	✓	✓
Max angle of view	Maximum angle that is created by the ball with any two adjacent opponent players	✓	✓
Max distance to opponents	Maximum Euclidean distance between adjacent opponent players in front of the ball holder	✓	✓
Min distance to teammates	Minimum distance between the ball holder and any of the teammate players	✓	✓
Time remaining	Time remained from action occurrence to the end of match half	✓	✓
Goal difference	Actual difference between the expert team and opponent goals	✓	✓
Action result	Successful or unsuccessful	–	✓
Body ID	Is the action performed by head or body or foot?	-	✓
Height in case of a pass	Ground, high, low	–	✓
Technique in case of a pass	In/out swinging, straight, through-ball	–	✓

interpret it as follows: we expect the team to score xPP sum goals on average of all penetrative passes in the games. Note that this value cannot be used for team evaluation (i.e., the higher xPP sum does not imply the better performance of the team). However, we can compare this value with the actual number of goals the

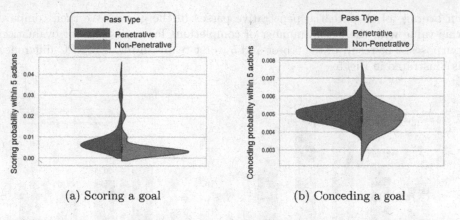

(a) Scoring a goal   (b) Conceding a goal

Fig. 3. Probability of scoring or conceding a goal within next 5 actions

team scored within the next 5 actions of a penetrative pass. Now the difference between actual goals and expectations implies the team performance, in which a positive xPP-difference indicates overperformance of the team to score a goal within the next 5 actions of a penetrative pass, and a negative xPP-difference indicates underperformance. Figure 4 illustrates the 5 best and 5 worst teams in terms of xPP-difference on left and right, respectively.

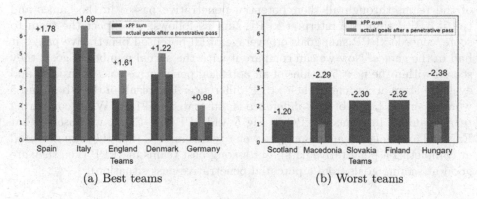

(a) Best teams   (b) Worst teams

Fig. 4. Teams' performance in converting a penetrative pass to a goal. Positive and negative numbers above the bars show the xPP-difference for each team.

xPC: Similarly, we evaluate the teams in terms of xPC (i.e., likelihood of successfully converting a potential penetrative pass to an actual penetrative pass). For this aim, we sum up all xPC of the teams through their potential penetrative pass situations and call it as xPC sum. We interpret an xPC sum for a team as follows: we expect the team to complete xPC sum penetrative passes on average of all potential penetrative passes in the games. We then compare this value with the actual number of completions for each team for evaluation purposes. The result of the 5 best and 5 worst teams in terms of xPC-difference is illustrated in Fig. 5.

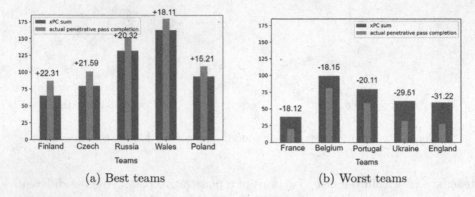

(a) Best teams   (b) Worst teams

Fig. 5. Teams' performance in completing a potential penetrative pass. Positive and negative numbers above the bars show the xPC-difference for each team.

xPPP: Finally, we evaluate the teams in terms of converting a potential penetrative pass into scoring/conceding situations. To do so, we sum up all xPPP of the teams through all their potential penetrative passes in the games and call it xPPP sum. We interpret xPPP sum as follows: we expect the team to score/concede xPPP sum goals on average of all potential penetrative passes it had in the games. Now we can compare it with the actual number of goals they scored within the next 5 actions of all potential penetrative pass situations, and evaluate them according to their xPPP-difference. The result of the 5 best and 5 worst teams in terms of xPP-difference is illustrated in Fig. 6. While comparing teams ranking in terms of xPC in Fig. 5 and xPPP in Fig. 6, we observe that England and Belgium are among the worst teams in xPC (i.e., they are not good at completing a penetrative pass), but among best teams in xPPP (i.e., they are good at scoring goals from a potential penetrative pass situation).

4.4   Field Section Analysis:

We also analyzed the impact of starting location of a potential penetrative pass to be a successful penetrative pass and how much we expect a potential penetrative pass to create a goal situation if it has been started in each field section along the touchline. To do so, we compute the $P3$ metric [13] as:

$$P3 = \frac{\text{number of successful penetrative passes}}{\text{number of potential penetrative passes}}$$

for each field section. Figure 7 illustrates the xPPP sum and the P3 for each one of the 5 sections of the field touchline (from 40 to 90 m, each section stretching

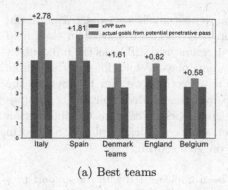
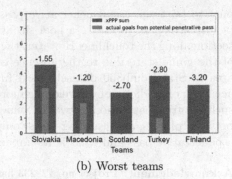

(a) Best teams (b) Worst teams

Fig. 6. Teams' performance in converting a potential penetrative pass to goal. Positive and negative numbers above the bars show the xPPP-difference for each team.

10 m). It can be noticed from Fig. 7a that a potential penetrative pass becomes successful more often in Sect. 4 and less often in Sect. 2. However, considering the xPPP sum graph in Fig. 7b we can observe that more goals are expected to be scored from a potential penetrative pass situation as we move forward in the field towards the opponent's goal.

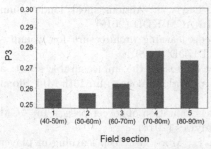
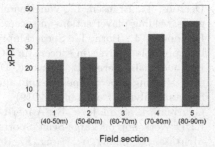

(a) P3% by Field touchline sections (b) xPPP sum by Field touchline sections

Fig. 7. Field section analysis on penetrative pass performance

5 Conclusion

Penetrative pass is an important tactic in offensive games. Being able to perform penetrative passes can lead the team in possession of the ball closer to scoring a goal. We proposed a possible application of event and positional data to measure teams' performance in terms of penetrative passes. For the best five and worst five teams in the dataset, we provide a trade-off between the ability to complete penetrative passes, and the expected value of goals they can create by doing so. Besides, we showed the impact of starting location of a potential penetrative pass to be a successful penetrative pass and how much we expect a potential penetrative pass to create a goal situation if it has been started in each field section along the touchline. However, the current study still lacks the full context of the game state due to the absence of some players' locations in the visible area of StatsBomb360 dataset. As a future direction, we aim to improve the accuracy of prediction by developing more sophisticated deep learning techniques such as graph attention networks, which could better capture the interaction between players, and use the results to infer what could lead a player to perform a penetrative pass and what is its impact on goal scoring.

Acknowledgment. Project no. 128233 has been implemented with the support provided by the Ministry of Innovation and Technology of Hungary from the National Research, Development and Innovation Fund, financed under the FK_18 funding scheme. We thank Hadi Sotudeh for his valuable comments that helped improve this paper.

References

1. How impactful are line-breaking passes? https://bit.ly/39uQe6Q
2. Bialkowski, A., Lucey, P., Carr, P., Yue, Y., Sridharan, S., Matthews, I.: Large-scale analysis of soccer matches using spatiotemporal tracking data. In: IEEE International Conference on Data Mining (ICDM) (2021)
3. Decroos, T., Bransen, L., Van Haaren, J., Davis, J.: Actions speak louder than goals: valuing player actions in soccer. In: In ACM KDD (2019)
4. Fernandez, J., Born, L.: SoccerMap: a deep learning architecture for visually-interpretable analysis in soccer. In: ECML PKDD (2020)
5. Fernandez, J., Bornn, L., Cervone, D.: Decomposing the immeasurable sport: a deep learning expected possession value framework for soccer. In: 13th MIT Sloan Sports Analytics Conference (2019)
6. Gyarmati, L., Stanojevic, R.: A merit-based evaluation of soccer passes. In: ACM KDD Workshop on Large-Scale Sports Analytics (2016)
7. Mehrasa, N., Zhong, Y., Tung, F., Bornn, L., Mori, G.: Deep learning of player trajectory representations for team activity analysis. In: 12th MIT Sloan Sports Analytics Conference (2018)
8. Peralta Alguacil, F., Fernandez, J., Piñones Arce, P., Sumpter, D.: Seeing in to the future: using self-propelled particle models to aid player decision-making in soccer. In: In Proceedings of the 14th MIT Sloan Sports Analytics Conference (2020)
9. Power, P., Ruiz, H., Wei, X., Lucey, P.: Not all passes are created equal: objectively measuring the risk and reward of passes in soccer. In: ACM KDD (2017)
10. Rahimian, P., Oroojlooy, A., Toka, L.: Towards optimized actions in critical situations of soccer games with deep reinforcement learning. In: IEEE DSAA (2021)
11. Rahimian, P., Van Haaren, J., Abzhanova, T., Toka, L.: Beyond action valuation: a deep reinforcement learning framework for optimizing player decisions in soccer. In: 16th MIT Sloan Sports Analytics Conference (2022)
12. Reina, R., Raabeb, D., Memmert, D.: Which pass is better? Novel approaches to assess passing effectiveness in elite soccer. Hum. Mov. Sci. **55**, 172–181 (2017)
13. Sotude, H.: Potential penetrative pass (P3). In: STASBOMB Conference (2021)

Evaluation of Creating Scoring Opportunities for Teammates in Soccer via Trajectory Prediction

Masakiyo Teranishi[1], Kazushi Tsutsui[1], Kazuya Takeda[1], and Keisuke Fujii[1,2,3(✉)]

[1] Graduate School of Informatics, Nagoya University, Nagoya, Japan
fujii@i.nagoya-u.ac.jp
[2] Center for Advanced Intelligence Project, RIKEN, Fukuoka, Japan
[3] PRESTO, Japan Science and Technology Agency, Saitama, Japan

Abstract. Evaluating the individual movements for teammates in soccer players is crucial for assessing teamwork, scouting, and fan engagement. It has been said that players in a 90-min game do not have the ball for about 87 min on average. However, it has remained difficult to evaluate an attacking player without receiving the ball, and to reveal how movement contributes to the creation of scoring opportunities for teammates. In this paper, we evaluate players who create off-ball scoring opportunities by comparing actual movements with the reference movements generated via trajectory prediction. First, we predict the trajectories of players using a graph variational recurrent neural network that can accurately model the relationship between players and predict the long-term trajectory. Next, based on the difference in the modified off-ball evaluation index between the actual and the predicted trajectory as a reference, we evaluate how the actual movement contributes to scoring opportunity compared to the predicted movement. For verification, we examined the relationship with the annual salary, the goals, and the rating in the game by experts for all games of a team in a professional soccer league in a year. The results show that the annual salary and the proposed indicator correlated significantly, which could not be explained by the existing indicators and goals. Our results suggest the effectiveness of the proposed method as an indicator for a player without the ball to create a scoring chance for teammates.

Keywords: Multi-agent · Deep learning · Trajectory · Sports · Football

1 Introduction

Assessing the movements of individual players for teammates in team sports is an important aspect of building teamwork, assessment of players' salaries, player recruitment, and scouting. In soccer, most analytics has focused on the outcomes of discrete events near the ball (on-ball) [4, 11, 13, 33–35, 40, 41] whereas much of the importance in player movements exist in the events without the ball (off-ball). For example, it is said that players in a 90-min game do not have the ball for about 87 min on average [16]. However, continuous off-ball movements are usually not discretized and difficult to understand except for core fans, experienced players, and coaches. Also for the media and building fan engagement, quantitative evaluation of off-ball players is an issue in

© The Author(s), under exclusive license to Springer Nature Switzerland AG 2023
U. Brefeld et al. (Eds.): MLSA 2022, CCIS 1783, pp. 53–73, 2023.
https://doi.org/10.1007/978-3-031-27527-2_5

demand, which provides a common reference for beginners and experts in the sport e.g., when arguing a play of a favorite player.

Regarding the off-ball player evaluation methods, the positioning itself related to the goal was evaluated from the location data of all players and the ball. For example, the method called off-ball scoring opportunity (OBSO) to evaluate the player who receives the ball [46] and the method to evaluate the movement to create space [16] have been proposed. However, it has been still difficult to clarify how movements contribute to the creation of scoring opportunities for teammates, to evaluate other attacking players who do not receive it (e.g., a player moving tactically for teammates), and often to evaluate a score prediction to reflect the position of the multiple defenders.

In this paper, we propose a new evaluation indicator, Creating Off-Ball Scoring Opportunity (C-OBSO in Fig. 1A), aiming for evaluating players who create scoring opportunities when the attacking player is without the ball. (i) First, we modify the score model in the framework of OBSO [46] with the potential score model that reflects the positions of multiple defenders with a mixed Gaussian distribution (Fig. 1B). (ii) Next, we accurately model the relationship between athletes and perform long-term trajectory predictions (Fig. 1A) using the graph variational recurrent neural network (GVRNN) [52]. (iii) Finally, based on the difference in the modified off-ball evaluation index between the actual and the predicted trajectory (Fig. 1A), we evaluate how the actual movement contributes to scoring opportunity relative to the predicted movement as a reference.

In summary, our main contributions were as follows. (1) We proposed an evaluation method of how movements contributed to the creation of scoring opportunities compared to the predicted movements of off-ball players in team sports attacks. (2) As a score predictor, we proposed a potential score model that considers the positions of multiple defenders in a mixed Gaussian distribution. (3) In the experiment, we analyzed the relationship between the annual salary, the goals, and the game rating by experts, and show the effectiveness of the proposed method as an indicator for an off-ball player to create scoring opportunities for teammates. Our approach can evaluate continuous movements of players by comparing with the reference (here predicted) movements, which are difficult to be discretized or labeled but crucial for teamwork, scouting, and fan engagement. The structure of this paper is as follows. First, we overview the related works in Sect. 4 and present experimental results in Sect. 3. Next, we describe our methods in Sect. 2 and conclude this paper in Sect. 5.

2   Proposed Framework

Here, we propose C-OBSO based on the motivation to evaluate players who create off-ball scoring opportunities for teammates. To this end, in Sect. 2.1, we first propose a potential score model that reflects the positions of multiple defenders with a mixed Gaussian distribution. Next, in Sect. 2.2, we predict multi-agent trajectory using GVRNN [52] and evaluate the difference between the actual value of the modified OBSO and the predicted value (as a reference) to evaluate how the movement contributed to the creation of scoring opportunities.

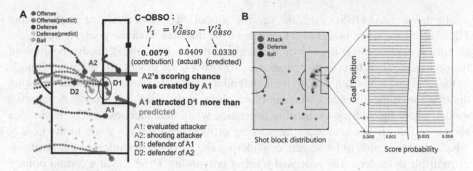

Fig. 1. Our C-OBSO example and potential score model. (A) Example of C-OBSO computation. A1 is the player to be finally evaluated, A2 is the shooting player, D1 and D2 are the defender of A1 and A2, respectively. V_1 is the C-OBSO value of A1, V_{OBSO}^2 is the actual OBSO, and $V_{OBSO}'^2$ is the reference OBSO value of A2 using the predicted trajectory. (B) Potential score model. Left: shot-blocking distribution formed by defenders. Right: shot probability corresponding to each shot vector. The vertical axis is the goal position (m), and the horizontal axis is the shot probability corresponding to each shot vector.

2.1 Potential Score Model in Modified OBSO

First, we describe the base model of our evaluation method called OBSO [46] and then propose the potential score model. OBSO evaluates off-ball players by computing the following joint probability

$$P(G|D) = \Sigma_{r \in R \times R} P(S_r \cap C_r \cap T_r|D) \tag{1}$$
$$= \Sigma_r P(S_r|C_r, T_r, D)P(C_r|T_r, D)P(T_r|D), \tag{2}$$

where D is the instantaneous state of the game (e.g., player positions and velocities). The details in OBSO are given in Appendix B. $P(S_r)$ is the probability of scoring from an arbitrary point $r \in R \times R$ on the pitch, assuming the next on-ball event occurs there. $P(C_r)$ is the probability that the passing team will control a ball at point r. $P(T_r)$ is the probability that the next on-ball event occurs at point r. Here, for simplicity, we can assume that $P(S_r|D), P(T_r|D), P(C_r|D)$ are independent if the parameter $\alpha = 0$ in the original work implementation (Eq. (6) in [46]). Then, the joint probability can be decomposed into a series of conditional probabilities as follows:

$$P(G|D) = \Sigma_{r \in R \times R} P(S_r|D)P(C_r|D)P(T_r|D). \tag{3}$$

$P(C_r|D)$ is the probability that the attacking team will control the ball at point r assuming the next on-ball event occurs there, which is called the potential pitch control field (PPCF). $P(T_r|D)$ is defined as a two-dimensional Gaussian distribution with the current ball coordinates as the mean. $P(S_r|D)$ is simply calculated as a value that decreases with the distance from the goal. We used the grid data and computed $P(C_r|D)$ and $P(T_r|D)$ based on the code at https://github.com/Friends-of-Tracking-Data-FoTD/LaurieOnTracking.

In the original OBSO [46], the scoring probability was calculated as the output $P(S_r|D)$ of the score model as a function of the distance from the goal. However, the scoring probability may depend on the angle to the goal and the defensive position of the opponent. Therefore, in this paper, we propose a score model that reflects the angle to the goal and the position of multiple defenders. Here, we consider the shot-blocking distribution of the defenders who can block shots in the field, and propose a potential model where the scoring probability decreases when defenders exist. The basic idea shown in Fig. 1B is to calculate the scoring probability from the angle to the goal at which the shot tends to be scored, considering the mixed distribution of the positions of multiple defenders. The proposed scoring probability $P(S_r^p|D)$ at a certain point r is calculated as the sum of the shot value V_{shot} as follows:

$$P(S_r^p|D) = \sum_{i=1}^{n} V_{shot}(s_i), \tag{4}$$

$$V_{shot}(s) = C(c - V_{block}), \tag{5}$$

where n is determined by the angle from the shooting position to the goal, and s is a shot vector per degree (n is larger when the shot from the center and smaller from the side). The shot value V_{shot} is calculated by subtracting the shot block value V_{block} from a certain constant c (c, C are parameters determined from data to be adjusted so that $V_{shot} \geq 0$ and $P(S_r^p) \in [0, 1]$). Let V_{block} be the sum of the shot block distribution values along the shot vector s. The shot blocking distribution is the sum of the normal distributions (variance $\sigma^2 = 0.5 + l_d$) assigned to each defender on the goal side of the shooting position (shot blockable players using legs), where l_d is the distance between the shooting position and the defender. We consider that goalkeepers have a shot blocking distribution with twice the value of normal defenders because of a higher shot-blocking ability. Here, we assume that the block distribution is not changed with the distance from the ball. A defender near to the ball may affect the ball, but far players use the flight time of the ball for their movement. This formulation is left for future work.

2.2   C-OBSO with Trajectory Prediction

Here, we describe the base model of our trajectory prediction method called GVRNN [52] and then describe our C-OBSO framework. Our contribution here is to evaluate how the actual "off-ball" movement contributes to scoring opportunity compared to the predicted movement (or trajectory) as a reference. In our method, we use GVRNN [52], which is a VRNN [10] combined with a graph neural network (GNN [27]). For the details in VRNN and GVRNN, see Appendices C and D. In GVRNN, the graph encoder-decoder network models the relationship between players as a graph, which is one of the best performing models for predicting player trajectories in team sports [52]. This is a probabilistic model which can sample multiple possible trajectories.

Based on the trajectory prediction, we propose an evaluation index C-OBSO of players who create scoring opportunities for teammates. The basic idea is to evaluate an off-ball player from the difference in the modified OBSO values between the predicted and actual movements of the players. The C-OBSO value of a player i without the ball can be expressed as follows.

$$V_i = V_{OBSO}^k - V_{OBSO}'^k, \tag{6}$$

where the player k is the ball carrier who performs a final action (e.g., shot), V_{OBSO}^k is the modified OBSO in the actual game situation, and $V_{OBSO}'^k$ is the modified OBSO based on the predicted trajectory as a reference. For example, in Fig. 1A, C-OBSO is positive and the player to be evaluated (A1) contributes more to the shooter (A2) than the referenced (predicted) player. Specifically, A1 has created a more advantageous situation for A2 by attracting D1 more than expected. C-OBSO can evaluate a player in such situations with an interpretable value (i.e., the increase in scoring probability). Theoretically, if perfectly predicted, C-OBSO is always zero, but actually, if we apply this to a test data, the perfect prediction is impossible. In other words, we assume the imperfect trajectory prediction in this framework.

3 Experiments

In this section, we validate the proposed method of the potential score model, the trajectory prediction model (GVRNN), and the C-OBSO itself. For our implementation, the code is available at https://github.com/keisuke198619/C-OBSO.

3.1 Dataset

In this study, we used all 34 games data of Yokohama F Marinos in the Meiji J1 League 2019 season to perform specific player-level evaluations in limited data. Note that the tracking data for all players and timesteps were not publicly shared in such amounts. The dataset includes event data (i.e., labels of actions, e.g., passing and shooting, recorded 30 Hz and the simultaneous xy coordinates of the ball) and tracking data (i.e., xy coordinates of all players recorded 25 Hz) provided by Data Stadium Inc. The company was licensed to acquire this data and sell it to third parties, and it was guaranteed that the use of the data would not infringe on any rights of the players or teams. For annual salaries, we used the salaries of the same team (Yokohama) in 2019 [45] because they were different valuation criteria for different teams and the transfer of the players took place during the season. The goals for each player in each match were collected from [24]. The rating by experts in each match [44] was also used for verification, which was scored in 0.5 point increments with a maximum of 10 points.

3.2 Data Processing for Verification

We used the attacking data of Yokohama F Marinos for the test and those of the opponent teams for training the model or parameter fitting. Again, since the data was limited in this study, we split the data in such a way, and if we have more data, we can analyze all teams with the training data with the same team. Here we describe the processing of the potential score model, the trajectory prediction model, the C-OBSO, and their statistical analyses.

Potential Score Model. To validate the potential score model, the opponent's shots (345 shots, 34 goals) were used for fitting the parameters c and C, and Yokohama F Marinos' shots (494 shots, 59 goals) were used for verification. The parameters c, C of the potential score model were determined to be $c = 1.1$, $C = 1/150$ using the data of the opponents. The potential score model was verified by the root mean square error (RMSE) between the actual score and the calculated scoring probability. We compared the RMSE with that of a simple score model as a function of distance from the goal for implementing the original OBSO [46] (see also Sect. 2.1). Although there have been more holistic score models such as [1, 17], to fairly compare with our potential model as a component of the modified OBSO, we consider the simple score model as an appropriate baseline.

Trajectory Prediction Model. For the test data of trajectory prediction and C-OBSO, we used 412 shot scenes of Yokohama F Marinos (we selected the sequences of consecutive events and excluded too short events such as a free kick). The trajectory prediction model was trained using the opponents' data to generate "league average" trajectories. The tracking data were down-sampled 10 Hz (after prediction, up-sampled at the 25 Hz) based on [20]. To verify the accuracy of the long-term trajectory prediction, we set various time lengths (6, 8, 10, and 12 s) using mean trajectories in 10 samples. We divided into the opponent data for batch training (6 s: 94208 sequences, 8 s: 49152 sequences, 10 s: 33536 sequences, 12 s: 24320 sequences) and the validation (6 s: 10477 sequences, 8 s: 5479 sequences, 10 s: 3730 sequences, 12 s: 2721 sequences). Note that the end of all sequences was the moment of a shot. The input feature has 92 dimensions (the xy coordinates and the velocity of 22 players and the ball). During training, the model was trained based on the one-step prediction error of all combinations of the two attackers who invaded the attacking third. We simultaneously predicted the three players: one of the off-ball attackers and the defenders closest to each attacker. Note that we only consider the three players' interactions and ignore others' interactions, because the prediction error will increase if the numbers increase, and the increase of the predicted players is left for future work.

For the test data of the 412 sequences, the three relevant players and the attacker from the same criterion were predicted. At the inference, using 2 s sequences as burn-in period, we predicted the sequences for the subsequent time lengths (i.e., 4, 6, 8, and 10 s) by updating the estimated position and velocity (i.e., performed long-term prediction). For the training of the proposed and baseline models, we used the Adam optimizer [25] with a learning rate of 0.001 and 10 training epochs. We set the batchsize to 256. For the performance metrics, we used the endpoint error (mean absolute error: MAE) from the actual trajectory.

C-OBSO. To compute C-OBSO, predicted trajectories with 4 s (total 6 s) were used. This is because a longer prediction time will result in a larger prediction error, while a shorter prediction time will not make a difference in the evaluation of C-OBSO. Although the negative values of C-OBSO are also calculated by comparison with the reference, the negative values were calculated as 0, assuming that they may not have a negative effect on the behavioral players. This is because there were many situations with negative values in which the shooter's defender did not take an appropriate defensive position in the predicted trajectory.

Statistical Analysis. For the verification of C-OBSO, we examined the relationship with the annual salary, the goals, and the expert's rating. Note that there is no ground truth available for the verification. We also compared them with the existing OBSO [46]. Since some of the data often did not follow normal distributions, we used Spearman's rank correlation coefficient ρ for these relationships. Regarding the RMSE in the potential score model and MAE in the trajectory prediction, for the same reason, we used nonparametric statistical tests to compare with the baselines. Regarding the potential score model, we used the Wilcoxon rank sum test. For all statistical calculations, $p < 0.05$ was considered as significant.

3.3   Our Model Verification

First, we validated the potential score model needed to calculate the C-OBSO. The RMSE with the actual scores was 0.324 ± 0.014 for the conventional score model [46] without considering the defenders and goal angles, and 0.309 ± 0.0014 for the potential score model ($p < 10^{-10}$). This result suggests that the proposed method models the scores more accurately.

Figure 2 shows an example of the two methods in two actual situations where a shot is attempted from a similar distance. In the existing method, the probabilities were the same (both 0.1237) because the shots were taken from almost the same distance. The proposed method had a lower scoring probability with more defenders (upper: 0.0489, lower: 0.1202). We indicate that the proposed method reflects the position of multiple defenders and can model the score accurately.

Next, we show the results of the trajectory prediction model for computing C-OBSO. Endpoint errors (MAE and standard error, [m]) in GVRNN were $0.608 \pm 0.014, 0.867 \pm 0.022, 1.701 \pm 0.045, 1.606 \pm 0.042$ in 4, 6, 8, 10 s prediction. In GVRNN, longer predictions show larger prediction errors except for the difference between 8 s and 10 s. Since the 4 s prediction of GVRNN achieved a low the MAE of less than 0.7 m, the GVRNN trajectory prediction of 4 s was used in the next C-OBSO. For details, see also Appendix E.

3.4   C-OBSO Results

Verification of C-OBSO is challenging because of no ground truth values or player ratings. Therefore, we analyzed the relationship with the annual salary, the goals, and the game rating by experts, whereas we admit that these variables include various confounding factors. The relationships between the average C-OBSO and OBSO values of each player of Yokohama F Marinos in 2019 and the annual salary of each player in 2019 are shown in Fig. 3 (note that the tracking data for all players and timesteps were not publicly shared). Here we analyzed 15 players with more than 10 sequences under evaluation. As a result, there was a significant positive correlation between annual salary

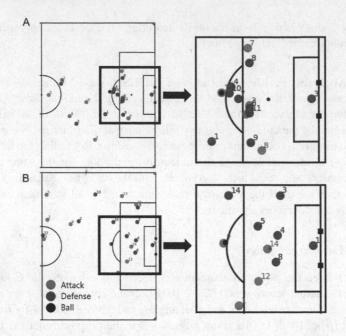

Fig. 2. Comparison between the score model of conventional and the proposed potential model. The scoring probability of our model is lower (A) when the defenders are crowded than (B), whereas that of the conventional score model in (A) was the same as (B).

and C-OBSO ($\rho = 0.45, p = 0.046$). In addition, the two players with the higher evaluation values but lower salaries (in red in Fig. 3A) were highly evaluated players, who won the individual awards (the most valuable player and valuable player award). In fact, their annual salary for the following year (2020) was also increased (valuable player: increased from 11 million yen to 40 million yen; the most valuable player: increased from 20 million yen to 60 million yen).

We found that these tendencies were similar to the C-OBSO and OBSO without the potential score model (see Appendix F). On the other hand, there was no significant correlation ($\rho = -0.28, p = 0.154$) for OBSO, which evaluates a player's own scoring opportunities (Fig. 3B). We also examined the relationship between annual salary and goals (Fig. 3C), and found no significant correlation ($\rho = -0.23, p = 0.208$). Therefore, there was no relationship between annual salary and goals. There were many players with zero goals, and it is difficult to evaluate them only with the goals.

Next, in order to examine the relationship with player performance in more detail, we show the relationship between C-OBSO and the rating by experts of the top three scorers (Nakagawa with 15 goals, Marcos with 15 goals, and Edigar with 11 goals in this season) in Fig. 4. We analyzed the games in which there were two or more C-OBSO evaluations using the average of C-OBSO values on each game (17 games for Nakagawa, 14 games for Marcos, and 10 games for Edigar). A strong positive correlation was found only for Nakagawa ($\rho = 0.75, p = 0.0003$) but not for Marcos ($\rho = 0.27, p = 0.174$) and Edigar ($\rho = -0.37, p = 0.145$). In Appendix G, we show

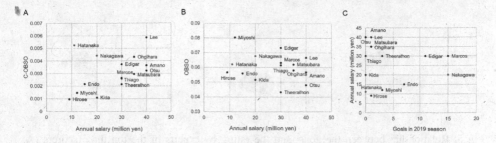

Fig. 3. Relationship between indicators, goal, and annual salary in a team. (A) Relationship between C-OBSO and the salary. (B) Relationship between OBSO [46] and the salary. (C) Relationship between each player's goals and annual salary. Red players received individual awards (Hatanaka: valuable player Award, Nakagawa: the most valuable player award).

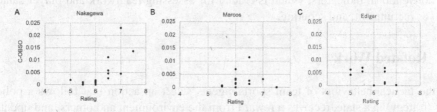

Fig. 4. Relationship between C-OBSO and the rating by experts of the top three scorers (A: Nakagawa, B: Marcos, C: Edigar) for each game.

the results of the other four players who played seven games or more and had two related scoring opportunities or more (for C-OBSO). Similarly, there were no significant correlations between them for all players ($ps < 0.190$, $ps > 0.05$). In addition to the number of scoring opportunities for teammates (17 times), the results found that Nakagawa would be subjectively and quantitatively an outstanding player.

For reference, we also show the relationship between the goals of the top three scorers and the ratings by experts in Fig. 5. We analyzed the games in which each player played (33 games for Nakagawa, 33 for Marcos, and 16 for Edigar). For each player, there were strong correlations between the goals and the rating (Nakagawa $\rho = 0.63, p = 4.33 \times 10^{-5}$, Marcos $\rho = 0.71, p = 1.98 \times 10^{-6}$, Edigar $\rho = 0.91, p = 4.40 \times 10^{-7}$). We found that the rating of each game depends on a rare event (i.e., goals). In Appendix G, we show the results of the other four players who scored two points or more. Similarly, there were significant correlations between them for all players ($ps > 0.516$, $ps < 0.018$). Recall that there was a stronger correlation between C-OBSO and Nakagawa's rating than for the other two players. Nakagawa also had higher average ratings than the other players (6.26 for Nakagawa, 5.97 for Marcos, and 6.09 for Edigar), and he was the player who won the most valuable player award. The game rating by experts would depend on the goals, but it may also evaluate the creation of scoring opportunities only for Nakagawa. From these results, we speculate that Nakagawa was highly evaluated not only for his scoring but also for his contribution to other attacking players. Our method can also evaluate players difficult to be evaluated

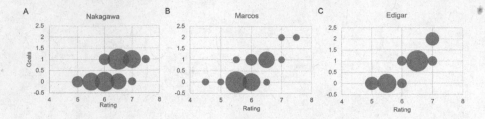

Fig. 5. Relationship between the goals and the rating by experts of the top three scorers (A: Nakagawa, B: Marcos, C: Edigar) for each game. The size of the circle represents the frequency because there are many combinations of the goals and the rating with the same value.

by conventional indicators, which is crucial for assessing teamwork and player salary, player recruitment, and scouting.

4   Related Work

In the tactical behaviors of team sports, agents select an action that follows a policy (or strategy) in a state, receives a reward from the environment and others, and updates the state [19]. This is similar to a reinforcement learning framework (e.g., [3]). Due to the difficulty in modeling the entire framework from data for various reasons [50] (e.g., a sparse reward and difficulty in estimating intents), we can adopt two approaches: to estimate the related variables and functions from data (i.e., inverse approach) as a sub-problem, and to build a model (e.g., reinforcement learning model) to generate data in virtual space (i.e., forward approach, e.g., [28,42]). Here, we focus on the former approach and introduce the research from the view of inverse approaches.

There have been many approaches to quantitatively evaluate the actions of attacking players about the scoring, such as based on the expected scores using tracking data [4,13,35,40,41], action data such as dribbling and passing [11,15], and estimating state-action value function (Q-function) [33,34,51]. Some researchers have evaluated passes [5,14,37], and others evaluated actions to receive a ball by assigning a value to the location with the highest expected score [32,46] and a rule-based manner [22]. In particular, Spearman [46] proposed an evaluation metric called OBSO to evaluate behavior based on location data and rule-based modeling. Defensive behaviors have also been evaluated based on data-driven [39,49] and rule-based manners (e.g., [48]). However, these score evaluations do not often reflect the position of multiple defenders and goal angles in rule-based manner.

From the perspective of reinforcement learning, there have been many studies on inverse approaches. As for the study of state evaluation, there are several studies based on score expectation (e.g., [7,8,17]) and based on the value of space (e.g., [6,16]). There is also research on estimating reward functions by inverse reinforcement learning [36,38]. Researchers performed trajectory prediction sometimes in terms of the policy function estimation, as imitation learning [20,29,30,48] and behavioral modeling [21,31,52,54] to mimic (not optimize) the policy using neural network approaches. In this paper, we first propose a method to evaluate how the actual "off-ball" movement contributes to scoring opportunity based on the difference between the state values generated from the actual and the reference policies.

5 Conclusion

In this paper, we evaluated players who create off-ball scoring opportunities by comparing actual movements with the reference movements generated by trajectory prediction. Our results suggest the effectiveness of the proposed method as an indicator for a player without the ball to create scoring opportunities for teammates. For future work, although the number of players to be evaluated was determined in the minimum setting, it is possible to evaluate the contribution to the scoring opportunities for teammates in a less limited way by predicting a larger number of players in both offense and defense. Furthermore, since our method evaluates off-ball players by comparing them with the referenced trajectory, the value becomes too small. Computing the evaluation value in a more interpretable way (e.g., in a score scale) would be future work. Finally, computing our indicators from broadcast videos (e.g., [12]) or other videos (e.g., top- or side-view [43]) would also be future work.

Acknowledgments. This work was supported by JSPS KAKENHI (Grant Numbers 20H04075 and 21H05300) and JST Presto (Grant Number JPMJPR20CA).

Appendix

A   Overview of our Method

The overview of our method is shown in the Fig. 6. (i) First, we modify the score model in the framework of OBSO [46] with the potential score model that reflects the positions of multiple defenders with a mixed Gaussian distribution (Fig. 1B). (ii) Next, we accurately model the relationship between athletes and perform long-term trajectory predictions (Fig. 1A) using the graph variational recurrent neural network (GVRNN) [52]. (iii) Finally, based on the difference in the modified off-ball evaluation index between the actual and the predicted trajectory (Fig. 1A), we evaluate how the actual movement contributes to scoring opportunity relative to the predicted movement as a reference.

B   Off-Ball Scoring Opportunity [46]

Here, we describe the base model of our evaluation method called OBSO [46]. OBSO evaluates off-ball players by computing the following joint probability

$$P(G|D) = \Sigma_{r \in R \times R} P(S_r \cap C_r \cap T_r | D) \tag{7}$$
$$= \Sigma_r P(S_r | C_r, T_r, D) P(C_r | T_r, D) P(T_r | D), \tag{8}$$

where D is the instantaneous state of the game (e.g., player positions and velocities). $P(S_r)$ is the probability of scoring from an arbitrary point $r \in R \times R$ on

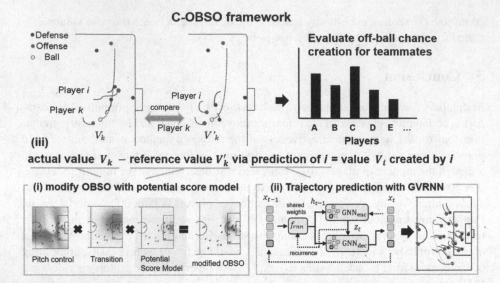

Fig. 6. Overview of our method. (i) First, we propose a potential score model to improve OBSO [46]. (ii) We then predict players' trajectories using GVRNN [52] to generate a reference player trajectory. (iii) Finally, the proposed C-OBSO is calculated by the difference between the evaluation value in the actual game situation and the referenced or predicted game situation.

the pitch, assuming the next on-ball event occurs there. $P(C_r)$ is the probability that the passing team will control a ball at point r. $P(T_r)$ is the probability that the next on-ball event occurs at point r. Here, for simplicity, we can assume that $P(S_r|D), P(T_r|D), P(C_r|D)$ are independent if the parameter $\alpha = 0$ in the original work implementation (Eq. (6) in [46]). Then, the joint probability can be decomposed into a series of conditional probabilities as follows:

$$P(G|D) = \Sigma_{r \in R \times R} P(S_r|D) P(C_r|D) P(T_r|D). \qquad (9)$$

We show the illustrative example of OBSO in Fig. 7. $P(C_r|D)$ is the probability that the attacking team will control the ball at point r assuming the next on-ball event occurs there, which is called the potential pitch control field (PPCF). $P(T_r|D)$ is defined as a two-dimensional Gaussian distribution with the current ball coordinates as the mean. The standard deviation is set to 14 m, which is the average distance of the next event [46]. $P(S_r|D)$ is simply calculated as a value that decreases with the distance from the goal. We used the grid data and computed $P(C_r|D)$ and $P(T_r|D)$ based on the code at https://github.com/Friends-of-Tracking-Data-FoTD/LaurieOnTracking.

Although $P(T_r|D)$ and $P(S_r|D)$ are simple functions, we need to explain $P(C_r|D)$ (PPCF) in more detail. PPCF [46] (a previous version is [47]) assumes that a player's ability to make a controlled touch on the ball (when near the ball) can be treated as a Poisson point process. That is, the longer a player is near the ball without another player interfering, the more likely it becomes that they can make a controlled touch on the ball. The model quantifies the probability of control for each player at each location on the pitch. The differential equation used to compute the control probability for each player at a specified location r at time t is:

$$\frac{dPPCF_j(t,r,T|s,\lambda_j)}{dT} = \left(1 - \sum_k PPCF_k(t,r,T|s,\lambda_j)\right) f_j(t,r,T|s)\lambda_j, \quad (10)$$

where $f_j(t,r,T|s)$ represents the probability that player j at time t can reach location r within time T. The parameter s is the temporal uncertainty of player-ball intercept time (has units of s), which is used in $f_j(t,r,T|s)$ (we set $s = 0.45$ based on [47]). The parameter λ_j is the rate of control representing the inverse of the mean time (has units of $1/s$) which would take a player to make a controlled touch on the ball. Conceptually, we consider the probability that player j will be able to control the ball during time T to $T + dT$ with the decay rate $f_j(t,r,T|s)\lambda_j$. We set $PPCF_j(t,r,T|s,\lambda_j) = 0$ for the attacking or defending team if the opponent team can arrive significantly before the attacking or defending team. By integrating Eq. (10) over T from 0 to ∞, we obtain a per-player probability of control. We integrate it over the players of the attacking team. $f_j(t,r,T|s)$ is represented as a logistic function such that

$$f_j(t,r,T|s) = \left[1 + \exp\left(-\frac{T - \tau_{exp}(t,r)}{\sqrt{3}s/\pi}\right)\right]^{-1}, \quad (11)$$

where $\tau_{exp}(t,r)$ is a expected intercept time computed from the location and velocity of the player j (including other constants, see [46] for the details). Conceptually, if

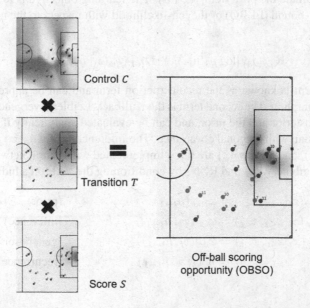

Control C

Transition T

Score S

Off-ball scoring
opportunity (OBSO)

Fig. 7. Off-ball scoring opportunities (OBSO) [46]: an evaluation index for scoring opportunities in the off-ball state. The OBSO on the right is calculated by the joint probability of control, transition, and score probability.

$T - \tau_{exp}(t, r) \geq 0$, the player will tend to intercept the ball and a temporal uncertainty $\sqrt{3}s/\pi$ is assumed. For the control rate parameter λ_j, higher values of λ_j mean less time is required before the player can control the ball. We set $\lambda_j = 4.3$ based on [47].

C   Variational Recurrent Neural Network [10]

In this section, we briefly overview recurrent neural networks (RNNs), variational autoencoders (VAEs), and variational RNNs (VRNNs).

From the perspective of a probabilistic generative model, an RNN models the conditional probabilities with a hidden state h_t that summarizes the past history in the first $t - 1$ timesteps:

$$p_\theta(x_t|x_{<t}) = \varphi(h_{t-1}), \qquad h_t = f(x_t, h_{t-1}), \tag{12}$$

where φ maps the hidden state to a probability distribution over states and f is a deterministic function such as LSTMs or GRUs. RNNs with simple output distributions often struggle to capture highly variable and structured sequential data. Recent work in sequential generative models addresses this issue by injecting stochastic latent variables into the model and using amortized variational inference to infer latent variables from data. VRNNs [10] is one of the methods using this idea and combining RNNs and VAEs.

VAE [26] is a generative model for non-sequential data that injects latent variables z into the joint distribution $p_\theta(a, z)$ and introduces an inference network parameterized by ϕ to approximate the posterior $q_\phi(z \mid a)$. The learning objective is to maximize the evidence lower-bound (ELBO) of the log-likelihood with respect to the model parameters θ and ϕ:

$$\mathbb{E}_{q_\phi(z|a)} [\log p_\theta(a|z)] - D_{KL}(q_\phi(z \mid a)||p_\theta(z)) \tag{13}$$

The first term is known as the reconstruction term and can be approximated with Monte Carlo sampling. The second term is the Kullback-Leibler divergence between the approximate posterior and the prior, and can be evaluated analytically if both distributions are Gaussian with diagonal covariance. The inference model $q_\phi(z \mid a)$, generative model $p_\theta(a \mid z)$, and prior $p_\theta(z)$ are often implemented with neural networks.

VRNNs combine VAEs and RNNs by conditioning the VAE on a hidden state h_t:

$$p_\theta(z_t|x_{<t}, z_{<t}) = \varphi_{\text{prior}}(h_{t-1}) \qquad \text{(prior)} \tag{14}$$

$$q_\phi(z_t|x_{\leq t}, z_{<t}) = \varphi_{\text{enc}}(x_t, h_{t-1}) \qquad \text{(inference)} \tag{15}$$

$$p_\theta(x_t|z_{\leq t}, x_{<t}) = \varphi_{\text{dec}}(z_t, h_{t-1}) \qquad \text{(generation)} \tag{16}$$

$$h_t = f(x_t, z_t, h_{t-1}). \qquad \text{(recurrence)} \tag{17}$$

VRNNs are also trained by maximizing the ELBO, which can be interpreted as the sum of VAE ELBOs over each timestep of the sequence:

$$\mathbb{E}_{q_\phi(z_{\leq T}|x_{\leq T})} \left[\sum_{t=1}^{T} \log p_\theta(x_t \mid z_{\leq T}, x_{<t}) \right.$$

$$\left. - D_{KL}\Big(q_\phi(z_t \mid x_{\leq T}, z_{<t}) \| p_\theta(z_t \mid x_{<t}, z_{<t})\Big) \right] \tag{18}$$

Note that the prior distribution of latent variable z_t depends on the history of states and latent variables (Eq. (14)).

D   Graph Variational Recurrent Neural Network [52]

Here, we briefly describe VRNN, GNN, and GVRNN.

In general, RNNs with simple output distributions often struggle to capture highly variable and structured sequential data (e.g., multimodal behaviors) [54]. Recent work in sequential generative models addressed this issue by injecting stochastic latent variables into the model and optimization using amortized variational inference to learn the latent variables (e.g., [10,18,23]). Among these methods, a variational RNN (VRNN) [10] has been widely used in base models for multi-agent trajectories [20,52,54] with unknown governing equations. A VRNN is essentially a variational autoencoder (VAE) conditioned on the hidden state of an RNN and is trained by maximizing the (sequential) evidence lower-bound (ELBO), described in Appendix A.

Next, we overview a graph neural network (GNN) based on [27]. Let v_k be a feature vector for each node k of K agents. Next, a feature vector for each edge $e_{(k,j)}$ is computed based on the nodes to which it is connected. The edge feature vectors are sent as "messages" to each of the connected nodes to compute their new output state o_k. Formally, a single round of message passing operations of a graph net is characterized below:

$$v \to e : e_{(k,j)} = f_e([v_k, v_j]), \tag{19}$$

$$e \to v : \quad o_i = f_v \left(\sum_{j \in N(k)} e_{(k,j)} \right), \tag{20}$$

where $N(k)$ is the set of neighbors of node k, and f_e and f_v are neural networks. In summary, a GNN takes in feature vectors $v_{1:K}$ and outputs a vector for each node $o_{1:K}$, i.e., $o_{1:K} = \text{GNN}(v_{1:K})$. The operations of the GNN satisfy the permutation equivariance property as the edge construction is symmetric between pairs of nodes and the summation operator ignores the ordering of the edges [53].

Next, we describe GVRNN [52], which models the interactions between them at each step using GNNs. Let $x_{\leq T} = \{x_1, \ldots, x_T\}$ denote a sequence of locations. In this paper, GVRNN update equations are as follows:

$$p_\theta(z_t|x_{<t}, z_{<t}) = \prod_k \mathcal{N}(z_{t,k}|\mu_{t,k}^{\text{pri}}, (\sigma_{t,k}^{\text{pri}})^2), \tag{21}$$

$$q_\phi(z_t|x_{\le t}, z_{<t}) = \prod_k \mathcal{N}(z_{t,k}|\mu_{t,k}^{\text{enc}}, (\sigma_{t,k}^{\text{enc}})^2), \tag{22}$$

$$p_\theta(x_t|z_{\le t}, x_{<t}) = \prod_k \mathcal{N}(z_{t,k}|\mu_{t,k}^{\text{dec}}, (\sigma_{t,k}^{\text{dec}})^2), \tag{23}$$

$$h_{t,k} = f_{rnn}(x_{t,k}, z_{t,k}, h_{t-1,k}). \tag{24}$$

where h_t and z_t are deterministic and stochastic latent variables. $p_\theta(x_t \mid z_{\le t}, x_{<t})$, $q_\phi(z_t \mid x_{\le t}, z_{<t})$, and $p_\theta(z_t \mid x_{<t}, z_{<t})$ are generative model, the approximate posterior or inference model, and the prior model, respectively. $\mathcal{N}(\cdot|\mu, \sigma^2)$ denotes a multivariate normal distribution with mean μ and covariance matrix $\text{diag}(\sigma^2)$, and

$$[\mu_{t,1:K}^{\text{pri}}, \sigma_{t,1:K}^{\text{pri}}] = \text{GNN}_{\text{pri}}(h_{t-1,1:K}), \tag{25}$$

$$[\mu_{t,1:K}^{\text{enc}}, \sigma_{t,1:K}^{\text{enc}}] = \text{GNN}_{\text{enc}}([x_{t,1:K}, h_{t-1,1:K}]), \tag{26}$$

$$[\mu_{t,1:K}^{\text{dec}}, \sigma_{t,1:K}^{\text{dec}}] = \text{GNN}_{\text{dec}}([z_{t,1:K}, h_{t-1,1:K}]). \tag{27}$$

The prior network GNN_{pri}, encoder GNN_{enc}, and decoder GNN_{dec} are GNNs with learnable parameters ϕ and θ. Here we used the mean value $\mu_{t+1,1:K}^{\text{dec}}$ as input variables $\hat{x}_{t+1}^{l'}$ in the following theory-based computation. GVRNN is trained by maximizing the sequential ELBO in a similar way to VRNN as described in Appendix C.

E   Validation Results of Trajectory Prediction Model

To verify the accuracy of the trajectory prediction model, We compared our approach with two baselines: VRNN [10] and RNN (RNN+Gauss) implemented using a gated recurrent unit (GRU) [9] and a decoder with Gaussian distribution for prediction [2].

For the MAE in the trajectory, to compare the various methods and time lengths, we first performed the Kruskal-Wallis test. As the post-hoc comparison, since we are interested in the differences from GVRNN (VRNN and RNN for four time lengths) and time lengths in GVRNN (4 and 6, 6 and 8, and 8 and 10 s), we performed the Wilcoxon rank sum test with Bonferroni correction such that the p-value was multiplied by 11 $(4 \times 2 + 3)$.

We show the results of the trajectory prediction model for computing C-OBSO. The endpoint errors (MAE) of the three players are shown in Table 1. In the statistical evaluation, there were significant differences in all classification performance and tasks $(p < 10^{-10})$ using the Kruskal-Wallis test. In the following evaluations, we indicate the post-hoc comparison results. The trajectory prediction model used in C-OBSO (GVRNN) shows a lower prediction error than other models $(ps < 10^{-10})$.

In GVRNN, longer predictions show larger prediction errors $(ps < 10^{-10})$ except for the difference between 8 s and 10 s $(p > 0.05)$. Note that we verified the existing GVRNN [52] performance, which uses a centralized optimization whereas VRNN and RNN+Gauss use the decentralized optimization (for each player). Since the 4 s prediction of GVRNN achieved a low the MAE of less than 0.7 m, the GVRNN trajectory prediction of 4 s was used in the next C-OBSO.

F   C-OBSO and OBSO Results Without the Potential Score Model

To investigate the effect of the potential model on the C-OBSO and OBSO computations, we also computed C-OBSO and OBSO results without the potential score model. Results shown in Fig. 8 were similar to those with the potential model, but there were no significant correlations between the C-OBSO and salary ($\rho = 0.38, p = 0.08$) and between the OBSO and salary ($\rho = -0.18, p = 0.26$).

Table 1. Trajectory prediction endpoint errors (MAE and standard error) in three methods.

	4 s	6 s	8 s	10 s
GVRNN	**0.608 ± 0.014**	**0.867 ± 0.022**	**1.701 ± 0.045**	**1.606 ± 0.042**
VRNN	5.952 ± 0.118	7.767 ± 0.160	9.127 ± 0.188	10.168 ± 0.225
RNN+Gauss	9.101 ± 0.144	11.396 ± 0.202	13.312 ± 0.245	15.327 ± 0.302

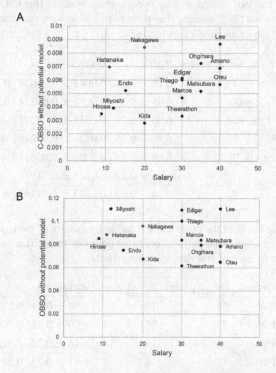

Fig. 8. Relationship between indicators without the potential score model and annual salary in a team. (A) Relationship between C-OBSO without the potential model and the salary. (B) Relationship between OBSO [46] without the potential model and the salary. Configurations are same as Fig. 3.

G   Relationship Between Rating, C-OBSO, and Goal

We additionally analyzed the relationship between the game rating by experts, C-OBSO, and the number of goals. First, we show the relationship between C-OBSO and the rating by experts of the top seven scorers in Table 2. We analyzed seven players who played seven games or more and had two related scoring opportunities or more (for C-OBSO). There were no significant correlations between them for all players ($\rho s < 0.190$, $ps > 0.05$) except for Nakagawa.

Next, we also show the relationship between the goals of the top seven scorers and the ratings by experts in Table 3. We analyzed the games in which each player scored two points or more. There were significant correlations between them for all players ($\rho s > 0.516$, $ps < 0.018$).

Table 2. Relationship between C-OBSO and the rating by experts of the top seven creator of scoring opportunities for teammate for each game. We analyzed seven players who played seven games or more and had two related scoring opportunities or more (for C-OBSO). The OBSO values were different from Fig. 3 because the values in this table were computed by the mean and standard deviation of the mean value of each game.

Name	Position	No. of games	Rating	C-OBSO	ρ	p
Nakagawa	FW	17	6.18 ± 0.64	0.0043 ± 0.00624	0.751	0.0003
Marcos	FW	14	6.05 ± 0.60	0.0032 ± 0.00324	0.272	0.1738
Edigar	FW	10	6.00 ± 0.71	0.0038 ± 0.00291	−0.371	0.1454
Endo	MF	7	5.86 ± 0.56	0.0020 ± 0.00248	−0.418	0.1751
Amano	MF	7	5.86 ± 0.38	0.0086 ± 0.00617	−0.116	0.4024
Ohgihara	MF	7	6.00 ± 0.29	0.0123 ± 0.01073	−0.134	0.3876
Matsubara	DF	7	6.14 ± 0.63	0.0079 ± 0.01335	0.189	0.3426

Table 3. Relationship between the goals and the rating by experts of the top seven scorers. We analyzed the games in which each player scored two points or more. The ratings were different from Table 2 because of the different data selection criteria.

Name	Position	No. of games	No. of goals	Rating	ρ	p
Nakagawa	FW	33	15	6.33 ± 0.79	0.630	4.33E-05
Marcos	FW	33	15	6.09 ± 0.92	0.709	1.98E-06
Edigar	FW	16	11	6.14 ± 0.75	0.912	4.40E-07
Erik	FW	12	8	6.13 ± 0.77	0.599	1.97E-02
Endo	MF	29	7	5.88 ± 0.61	0.613	2.03E-04
Theerathon	DF	25	3	5.88 ± 0.62	0.517	4.09E-03
Miyoshi	MF	16	3	6.03 ± 0.64	0.529	1.75E-02

References

1. Anzer, G., Bauer, P.: A goal scoring probability model for shots based on synchronized positional and event data in football (soccer). Front. Sports Active Living **3**, 53 (2021)
2. Becker, Stefan, Hug, Ronny, Hübner, Wolfgang, Arens, Michael: RED: a simple but effective baseline predictor for the *TrajNet* benchmark. In: Leal-Taixé, Laura, Roth, Stefan (eds.) ECCV 2018. LNCS, vol. 11131, pp. 138–153. Springer, Cham (2019). https://doi.org/10. 1007/978-3-030-11015-4_13
3. Bernstein, D.S., Givan, R., Immerman, N., Zilberstein, S.: The complexity of decentralized control of Markov decision processes. Math. Oper. Res. **27**(4), 819–840 (2002)
4. Bransen, Lotte, Van Haaren, Jan: Measuring football players' on-the-ball contributions from passes during games. In: Brefeld, Ulf, Davis, Jesse, Van Haaren, Jan, Zimmermann, Albrecht (eds.) MLSA 2018. LNCS (LNAI), vol. 11330, pp. 3–15. Springer, Cham (2019). https://doi. org/10.1007/978-3-030-17274-9_1
5. Brooks, J., Kerr, M., Guttag, J.: Developing a data-driven player ranking in soccer using predictive model weights. In: Proceedings of the 22nd ACM SIGKDD International Conference on Knowledge Discovery and Data Mining, pp. 49–55 (2016)
6. Cervone, D., Bornn, L., Goldsberry, K.: Nba court realty. In: 10th MIT Sloan Sports Analytics Conference (2016)
7. Cervone, D., D'Amour, A., Bornn, L., Goldsberry, K.: Pointwise: Predicting points and valuing decisions in real time with nba optical tracking data. In: Proceedings of the 8th MIT Sloan Sports Analytics Conference, Boston, MA, USA, vol. 28, p. 3 (2014)
8. Cervone, D., D'Amour, A., Bornn, L., Goldsberry, K.: A multiresolution stochastic process model for predicting basketball possession outcomes. J. Am. Stat. Assoc. **111**(514), 585–599 (2016)
9. Cho, K., Van Merriënboer, B., Bahdanau, D., Bengio, Y.: On the properties of neural machine translation: Encoder-decoder approaches. arXiv preprint arXiv:1409.1259 (2014)
10. Chung, J., Kastner, K., Dinh, L., Goel, K., Courville, A.C., Bengio, Y.: A recurrent latent variable model for sequential data. Adv. Neural. Inf. Process. Syst. **28**, 2980–2988 (2015)
11. Decroos, T., Bransen, L., Van Haaren, J., Davis, J.: Actions speak louder than goals: valuing player actions in soccer. In: KDD, pp. 1851–1861 (2019)
12. Deliege, A., et al.: Soccernet-v2: a dataset and benchmarks for holistic understanding of broadcast soccer videos. In: 7th International Workshop on Computer Vision in Sports (CVsports) at IEEE/CVF Conference on Computer Vision and Pattern Recognition (CVPR 2021), pp. 4508–4519 (2021)
13. Decroos, T., Dzyuba, V., Van Haaren, J., Davis, J.: Predicting soccer highlights from spatiotemporal match event streams. In: Proceedings of the AAAI Conference on Artificial Intelligence, vol. 31 (2017)
14. Dick, U., Link, D., Brefeld, U.: Who can receive the pass? a computational model for quantifying availability in soccer. Data Min. Knowl. Disc. **36**(3), 987–1014 (2022)
15. Dick, U., Tavakol, M., Brefeld, U.: Rating player actions in soccer. Frontiers in Sports and Active Living, p. 174 (2021)
16. Fernandez, J., Bornn, L.: Wide open spaces: a statistical technique for measuring space creation in professional soccer. In: 12th MIT Sloan Sports Analytics Conference (2018)
17. Fernández, J., Bornn, L., Cervone, D.: Decomposing the immeasurable sport: a deep learning expected possession value framework for soccer. In: 13th MIT Sloan Sports Analytics Conference (2019)
18. Fraccaro, M., Sønderby, S.K., Paquet, U., Winther, O.: Sequential neural models with stochastic layers. In: Advances in Neural Information Processing Systems 29, pp. 2199–2207 (2016)

19. Fujii, K.: Data-driven analysis for understanding team sports behaviors. J. Robot. Mechatronics **33**(3), 505–514 (2021)
20. Fujii, K., Takeishi, N., Kawahara, Y., Takeda, K.: Policy learning with partial observation and mechanical constraints for multi-person modeling. arXiv preprint arXiv:2007.03155 (2020)
21. Fujii, K., Takeuchi, K., Kuribayashi, A., Takeishi, N., Kawahara, Y., Takeda, K.: Estimating counterfactual treatment outcomes over time in complex multi-agent scenarios. arXiv preprint arXiv:2206.01900 (2022)
22. Fujii, K., et al.: Cognition and interpersonal coordination of patients with schizophrenia who have sports habits. PLoS ONE **15**(11), e0241863 (2020)
23. Goyal, A.G.A.P., Sordoni, A., Côté, M.A., Ke, N.R., Bengio, Y.: Z-forcing: training stochastic recurrent networks. In: Advances in Neural Information Processing Systems 30, pp. 6713–6723 (2017)
24. JLEAGUE: Jleague.jp 2019 data (2019). https://www.jleague.jp/stats/2019/goal.html
25. Kingma, D.P., Ba, J.: Adam: a method for stochastic optimization. In: International Conference on Learning Representations (2015)
26. Kingma, D.P., Welling, M.: Auto-encoding variational bayes. In: International Conference on Learning Representations (2014)
27. Kipf, T., Fetaya, E., Wang, K.C., Welling, M., Zemel, R.: Neural relational inference for interacting systems. In: International Conference on Machine Learning, pp. 2688–2697 (2018)
28. Kurach, K., et al.: Google research football: A novel reinforcement learning environment. In: Proceedings of the AAAI Conference on Artificial Intelligence, vol. 34, pp. 4501–4510 (2020)
29. Le, H.M., Carr, P., Yue, Y., Lucey, P.: Data-driven ghosting using deep imitation learning. In: Proceedings of MIT Sloan Sports Analytics Conference (2017)
30. Le, H.M., Yue, Y., Carr, P., Lucey, P.: Coordinated multi-agent imitation learning. In: Proceedings of the 34th International Conference on Machine Learning-Volume 70, pp. 1995–2003. JMLR. org (2017)
31. Li, L., et al.: Grin: generative relation and intention network for multi-agent trajectory prediction. In: DAdvances in Neural Information Processing Systems 34 (2021)
32. Link, D., Lang, S., Seidenschwarz, P.: Real time quantification of dangerousity in football using spatiotemporal tracking data. PLoS ONE **11**(12), e0168768 (2016)
33. Liu, G., Luo, Y., Schulte, O., Kharrat, T.: Deep soccer analytics: learning an action-value function for evaluating soccer players. Data Min. Knowl. Disc. **34**(5), 1531–1559 (2020). https://doi.org/10.1007/s10618-020-00705-9
34. Liu, G., Schulte, O.: Deep reinforcement learning in ice hockey for context-aware player evaluation. arXiv preprint arXiv:1805.11088 (2018)
35. Lucey, P., Bialkowski, A., Monfort, M., Carr, P., Matthews, I.: quality vs quantity: Improved shot prediction in soccer using strategic features from spatiotemporal data. In: Proceedings of MIT Sloan Sports Analytics Conference, pp. 1–9 (2014)
36. Luo, Y., Schulte, O., Poupart, P.: Inverse reinforcement learning for team sports: Valuing actions and players. In: Bessiere, C. (ed.) Proceedings of the Twenty-Ninth International Joint Conference on Artificial Intelligence, IJCAI-20, pp. 3356–3363. International Joint Conferences on Artificial Intelligence Organization (7 2020)
37. Power, P., Ruiz, H., Wei, X., Lucey, P.: Not all passes are created equal: Objectively measuring the risk and reward of passes in soccer from tracking data. In: KDD, pp. 1605–1613 (2017)
38. Rahimian, P., Toka, L.: Inferring the strategy of offensive and defensive play in soccer with inverse reinforcement learning. In: Machine Learning and Data Mining for Sports Analytics (MLSA 2018) in ECML-PKDD Workshop (2020)

39. Robberechts, P.: Valuing the art of pressing. In: Proceedings of the StatsBomb Innovation In Football Conference, pp. 1–11. StatsBomb (2019)
40. Routley, K., Schulte, O.: A Markov game model for valuing player actions in ice hockey. In: Proceedings of the Thirty-First Conference on Uncertainty in Artificial Intelligence, UAI 2015, pp. 782–791. AUAI Press, Arlington (2015)
41. Schulte, O., Khademi, M., Gholami, S., Zhao, Z., Javan, M., Desaulniers, P.: A Markov game model for valuing actions, locations, and team performance in ice hockey. Data Min. Knowl. Disc. **31**(6), 1735–1757 (2017)
42. Scott, A., Fujii, K., Onishi, M.: How does AI play football? an analysis of RL and real-world football strategies. In: 14th International Conference on Agents and Artificial Intelligence (ICAART 2022), vol. 1, pp. 42–52 (2022)
43. Scott, A., Uchida, I., Onishi, M., Kameda, Y., Fukui, K., Fujii, K.: Soccertrack: a dataset and tracking algorithm for soccer with fish-eye and drone videos. In: 8th International Workshop on Computer Vision in Sports (CVsports) at IEEE/CVF Conference on Computer Vision and Pattern Recognition (CVPR 2022), pp. 3569–3579 (2022)
44. Soccer-digest: Soccer digest web j1 rating (2019). https://www.soccerdigestweb.com
45. Soccer-Money.net: Soccer-money.net (2019). https://www.soccer-money.net
46. Spearman, W.: Beyond expected goals. In: Proceedings of the 12th MIT Sloan Sports Analytics Conference, pp. 1–17 (2018)
47. Spearman, W., Basye, A., Dick, G., Hotovy, R., Pop, P.: Physics-based modeling of pass probabilities in soccer. In: Proceeding of the 11th MIT Sloan Sports Analytics Conference (2017)
48. Teranishi, M., Fujii, K., Takeda, K.: Trajectory prediction with imitation learning reflecting defensive evaluation in team sports. In: 2020 IEEE 9th Global Conference on Consumer Electronics (GCCE), pp. 124–125. IEEE (2020)
49. Toda, K., Teranishi, M., Kushiro, K., Fujii, K.: Evaluation of soccer team defense based on prediction models of ball recovery and being attacked. PLoS ONE **17**(1), e0263051 (2022)
50. Van Roy, M., Robberechts, P., Yang, W.C., De Raedt, L., Davis, J.: Learning a Markov model for evaluating soccer decision making. In: Reinforcement Learning for Real Life (RL4RealLife) Workshop at ICML 2021 (2021)
51. Wang, J., Fox, I., Skaza, J., Linck, N., Singh, S., Wiens, J.: The advantage of doubling: a deep reinforcement learning approach to studying the double team in the nba. arXiv preprint arXiv:1803.02940 (2018)
52. Yeh, R.A., Schwing, A.G., Huang, J., Murphy, K.: Diverse generation for multi-agent sports games. In: The IEEE Conference on Computer Vision and Pattern Recognition (CVPR), June 2019
53. Zaheer, M., Kottur, S., Ravanbakhsh, S., Poczos, B., Salakhutdinov, R.R., Smola, A.J.: Deep sets. In: Advances in Neural Information Processing Systems 30 (2017)
54. Zhan, E., Zheng, S., Yue, Y., Sha, L., Lucey, P.: Generating multi-agent trajectories using programmatic weak supervision. In: International Conference on Learning Representations (2019)

Cost-Efficient and Bias-Robust Sports Player Tracking by Integrating GPS and Video

Hyunsung Kim[1] , Chang Jo Kim[1], Minchul Jeong[1], Jaechan Lee[1], Jinsung Yoon[1], and Sang-Ki Ko[1,2(✉)]

[1] Fitogether Inc., Seoul, South Korea
{hyunsung.kim,changjo.kim,minchul.jeong,jaechan.lee,
jinsung.yoon}@fitogether.com
[2] Kangwon National University, Chuncheon, South Korea
sangkiko@kangwon.ac.kr

Abstract. Player tracking data are now widely used in the sports industry to provide deeper insights to domain participants. Global positioning systems (GPS) and camera-based optical tracking systems (OTS) are two common tracking systems, but the former suffers from location biases and the latter requires either a heavy installment of multiple cameras or a lot of manual correction work. Overcoming these weaknesses of individual systems, we propose a framework for cost-efficient and bias-robust player tracking by integrating GPS and video data. We design a sophisticated filtering algorithm to selectively use the positional information from bounding boxes detected in the video and use the GPS data as a reliable tool for identifying the chosen boxes. Using the player identity and location information of these bounding boxes, we estimate and remove GPS biases in two steps to obtain unbiased player trajectories. We demonstrate that our algorithm precisely tracks players from video with the aid of GPS data even in poor conditions such as the presence of player occlusions and players outside the sight of cameras.

Keywords: Sports player tracking · Multiple object tracking · Global positioning system · Signal processing · GPS-OTS integration

1 Introduction

Data science has become a vital tool in many industries over the last few years, and the sports industry is no exception. There are two branches of data frequently used in sports: event data that contains information about ball-related events that happen during matches and tracking data that logs the locations of every player at a particular time scale. In dynamic team sports such as soccer, basketball, and ice hockey, player tracking data offers rich information such as off-the-ball movements and interaction between players, which can be overlooked in event data. Especially in soccer, player tracking data can be utilized in many application scenarios such as formation/role estimation [3,10,21], space control analysis [5,22,23], playing style identification [11], and fatigue/injury prediction [19,20].

U. Brefeld et al. (Eds.): MLSA 2022, CCIS 1783, pp. 74–86, 2023.
https://doi.org/10.1007/978-3-031-27527-2_6

During the last two decades, there have been different types of tracking systems proposed and successfully adopted in soccer, such as global positioning systems (GPS), local positioning systems (LPS), and multiple camera-based optical tracking systems (OTS). While GPS has been appreciated for its low cost and easy installment compared to others, it is generally perceived that GPS is more sensitive to measurement environments such as weather and stadium condition [14]. On the other hand, OTS offers more accurate tracking information if there are sufficiently many high-definition cameras placed around the pitch from different angles. However, it is not feasible to install OTS on every pitch, especially on training pitches and away stadiums. Moreover, it is also not easy to rely on a smaller number of cameras for reliable tracking in OTS as it results in lower-quality raw data and eventually requires a manual correction process.

In this paper, we propose a framework for cost-efficient and bias-robust player tracking by integrating GPS and video data. Considering that OTS is more accurate in terms of positional accuracy for well-conditioned frames, we design a sophisticated filtering algorithm to selectively use the positional information from bounding boxes (abbreviated to "bboxes" hereafter) detected in the video. Also, we use the GPS data as a reliable tool for assigning player identities to the chosen bboxes by minimum-cost matching between GPS and OTS trajectories. With the matched pairs of GPS and OTS trajectories, we estimate and remove GPS biases in two steps to get unbiased player trajectories. We empirically demonstrate that the proposed GPS-OTS hybrid system achieves a more reliable and robust tracking performance even with a few fixed cameras at a single spot. See Fig. 1 for an overview of the proposed framework.

The paper is organized as follows: in Sect. 2, we present the background knowledge and related work to help understand the context and motivation of our work. In Sect. 3, we explain our GPS-OTS hybrid tracking algorithm step-by-step. In Sect. 4, we provide experimental results to evaluate the proposed algorithm. Section 5 concludes the paper.

2   Related Work

2.1   Optical Player Tracking

Due to recent advances in deep learning-based computer vision technology, we can detect players quickly and accurately from soccer videos under various conditions such as broadcast, tactical-cam, and panoramic videos [6,8,12,26]. However, the problem of assigning correct identities (IDs) to detected players stays as a tough challenge to overcome. Hurault et al. [8] introduced a self-supervised tracking algorithm robust to low-resolution videos and changeable recording conditions. Theiner et al. [25] proposed an automated pipeline to extract players' positional data from soccer videos. Naik et al. [16] identified players and referees by their jersey color observed in bounding boxes, and assigned IDs to players using deep appearance descriptors. Theagarajan et al. [24] presented a unified system that tracks players, classifies their teams, identifies the player controlling the ball, and even generates tactical statistics (i.e., duration of ball possession, the number of successful passes, dribbles, steals, and so on) of players.

Note that the aforementioned studies suffer from the ID switching problem caused by incorrect player detection such as missing/false detections or indistinguishable players such as visually overlapped players or similar players.

2.2   GPS-Based Player Tracking

Many professional teams have been using GPS for player tracking to monitor players' physical performance metrics, such as total running distances, number of sprints, and workload levels [7]. In contrast to optical player tracking, GPS-based player tracking has the clear merit of maintaining players' IDs consistently throughout the playing time.

Along with the development of GPS technology, the validity and reliability of GPS have been continuously verified in many studies [1,2,7,15,18]. For instance, Akyildiz et al. [1] presented that GPS devices exhibit low reliability when evaluating the distances covered at different speed zones. In addition, they claimed that the positional accuracy of GPS is influenced by speed, type of displacement, and other external factors such as weather conditions, curved stadium roofs, and so on [2,18]. Linke et al. [14] compared the measurement accuracies of GPS, LPS, and OTS against the Vicon motion capture system as a reference. Experimental results show that OTS is closer to the reference data than GPS, while GPS shows higher agreement to the reference on velocity, acceleration/deceleration, and total distance covered.

2.3   GPS-OTS Integration Approach

Since the improvement of GPS and OTS, there have been several studies to compare and integrate these two tracking systems. Buchheit et al. [4] suggested the possibility of interchanging between the three different tracking systems: GPS, OTS, and LPS. Observations of movement information from each system were compared, and system calibration equations were provided. Pons et al. [17] made a comparison of physical indicators between GPS and OTS obtained from real soccer games and reported the high relevance of those two systems. In their follow-up research [18], they presented that a GPS device tends to show a larger number of accelerations/decelerations than OTS, while the distances covered during accelerations/decelerations were similar.

To our knowledge, there has been no approach to player tracking by integrating GPS and OTS. In this paper, we propose a novel GPS-OTS hybrid tracking system that complements weaknesses of one another and shows noticeable positional accuracy without any manual annotation.

3   Main Contributions

Given a sequence of GPS trajectories and bbox coordinates resulting from object detection in the video, our goal is to find accurate player trajectories by estimating and removing the GPS biases. Since we know neither the target a detected

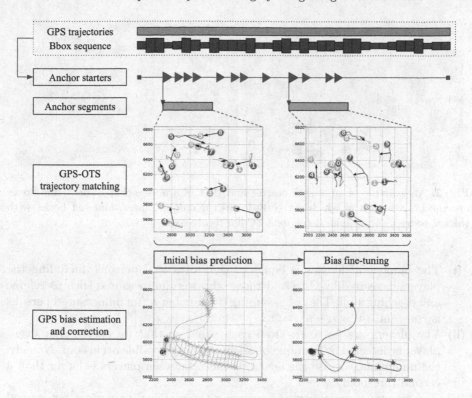

Fig. 1. Overview of the proposed algorithm.

bbox is tracking nor even whether it correctly locates an area occupied by a person, we first detect anchor segments where an algorithm can stably track bboxes of the same person in consecutive frames (Sects. 3.1 and 3.2). Then, we assign the player IDs of these bbox sequences, which we call OTS trajectories, by matching them with GPS trajectories (Sect. 3.3) in each anchor segment. Using the OTS trajectories with player ID information, we calculate and remove the GPS biases (Sect. 3.4). Lastly, these biases are fine-tuned for a final prediction of player locations (Sect. 3.5). See Fig. 1 for an overview of the proposed framework.

3.1 Anchor Starter Detection

First, we find *anchor starters* where every bbox correctly locates an actual person, and every person in the region of interest is detected as a bbox. For each frame t, we perform minimum-cost matching between the GPS coordinates $X^G(t) = \{\mathbf{x}_1^G(t), \ldots, \mathbf{x}_n^G(t)\}$ of players $p_1, \ldots, p_n$ and the bboxes $X^B(t) = \{\mathbf{x}_1^B(t), \ldots, \mathbf{x}_{m_t}^B(t)\}$ by Hungarian algorithm [13] with the sum of pairwise Euclidean distances as assignment cost. Note that m_t is the number of detected bboxes in frame t, and therefore varies across time. We regard a frame t as an anchor starter if it satisfies the following conditions:

Fig. 2. An example of an anchor starter and that of a non-anchor frame. Blue boxes are the bboxes each of which correctly locates a unique player, and red boxes with thicker edges indicate false detections. (Color figure online)

(i) The number of bboxes is equal to that of actual persons, including the players measured by GPS and those who were unmeasured such as referee and coaching staff. That is, assuming the number n^U of unmeasured persons is constant, $m_t = n + n^U =: m$.

(ii) The players are far apart from each other so that we ensure that every player is detected by a unique bbox by avoiding possible occlusions. Namely, the minimum pairwise Euclidean distance between players is larger than a certain threshold d_0.

(iii) The maximum assignment cost among the matched pairs does not exceed a threshold cost c_0, so we expect every player is detected by a bbox.

As a result, we sort out anchor starters $a_1, \ldots, a_K$ where each a_k for $1 \leq k \leq K$ satisfies that every $\mathbf{x}_i^G(a_k)$ is assigned to a unique bbox $\mathbf{x}_i^O(a_k) \in X^B(a_k)$. In other words, we find a permutation $(\mathbf{x}_1^O(a_k), \ldots, \mathbf{x}_m^O(a_k))$ of bboxes $\{\mathbf{x}_1^B(t), \ldots, \mathbf{x}_m^B(t)\}$ by the minimum cost matching with $(\mathbf{x}_1^G(a_k), \ldots, \mathbf{x}_n^G(a_k))$. (We place the unmatched bboxes in $(\mathbf{x}_{n+1}^O(a_k), \ldots, \mathbf{x}_m^O(a_k))$.) Fig. 2 shows two example frames where the first frame is an anchor starter and the second one is an ordinary (non-anchor) frame.

3.2   Anchor Segment Detection

At an anchor starter, there is a one-to-one correspondence between bboxes and actual persons in the region of interest. However, we cannot assure that the bbox $\mathbf{x}_i^O(t)$ locates the right player p_i, since GPS measurement has a bias and therefore incurs ID switches during the assignment process in Sect. 3.1.

To resolve these potential twists, we perform minimum-cost matching again in Sect. 3.3, but between trajectories instead of single points obtained from GPS and bboxes. To this end, we need to find *OTS trajectories*, each of which consists of a sequence of bboxes that tracks a unique person in the video. Considering that sorting out stable OTS trajectories lasting the entire playing time is almost impossible due to interspersed false positive and negative bboxes, we detect well-conditioned time intervals named *anchor segments* during which an algorithm can reliably find OTS trajectories.

Starting from each anchor starter a_k, we iterate over frames to construct an anchor segment $T_k = \{a_k, a_k + \Delta t, \ldots, a_k + l_k \Delta t\}$ and OTS trajectories $\mathbf{x}_i^O(T_k) = \{\mathbf{x}_i^O(t) \in X^B(t) : t \in T_k\}$ as follows:

(a) For the current frame at time t, find the minimum-cost matching between the OTS coordinates $\mathbf{x}_1^O(t), \ldots, \mathbf{x}_{m_t}^O(t)$ and the bboxes $\mathbf{x}_1^B(t + \Delta t), \ldots, \mathbf{x}_{m_{t+\Delta t}}^B(t + \Delta t)$ at the next frame. Note that the OTS coordinates $\mathbf{x}_1^O(a_k), \ldots, \mathbf{x}_m^O(a_k)$ at the anchor starter a_k are defined in Sect. 3.1.
(b) Check if $m_t = m_{t+\Delta t}$ and the maximum assignment cost does not exceed the certain threshold c_1. If so, append $t + \Delta t$ to the current anchor segment $\{a_k, a_k + \Delta t, \ldots, t\}$ and let $\mathbf{x}_i^O(t+\Delta t) \in X^B(t+\Delta t)$ be the bbox coordinate assigned to $\mathbf{x}_i^O(t)$ for each $1 \leq i \leq m_t$. Otherwise, terminate the iteration.

Considering that $T_{k+1} \subset T_k$ if an anchor segment starting from a_k reaches a_{k+1}, we skip the anchor starters in the middle of other anchor segments.

We now have OTS trajectories $X^O(T_k) = \{\mathbf{x}_1^O(T_k), \ldots, \mathbf{x}_m^O(T_k)\}$ where each sequence $\mathbf{x}_i^O(T_k)$ of bboxes follows a unique person in the video. The i-th OTS trajectory may not indicate the p_i in the video due to the aforementioned ID switches, which will be cleared up by the GPS-OTS trajectory matching in Sect. 3.3. Since too short trajectories are less robust against GPS biases, we only consider an anchor segment T_k to be *valid* if it lasts at least 1.0s.

3.3 GPS-OTS Trajectory Matching per Anchor Segment

Though GPS has a location bias varying across time, it accurately tracks the player's displacement [14]. In other words, though the GPS bias per frame may be significant, it fluctuates slowly along the time axis. Therefore, we propose GPS-OTS trajectory matching for the ID assignment rather than simply running the Hungarian algorithm independently for each frame as in Sect. 3.1.

Specifically, we perform minimum-cost matching between the GPS trajectories $\mathbf{x}_1^G(T_k), \ldots, \mathbf{x}_n^G(T_k)$ and the OTS trajectories $\mathbf{x}_1^O(T_k), \ldots, \mathbf{x}_m^O(T_k)$ per valid anchor segment T_k (with duration longer than or equal to 1.0 s). To be less affected by GPS biases, the Hungarian algorithm here uses a "shape-weighted" assignment cost that matches the trajectories with similar shapes rather than those just close to each other. That is, we define the center cost and the shape cost between a pair of trajectories, and set the assignment cost to a weighted sum of these two types of costs.

To put it concretely, we first get a sequence of differences and its mean by

$$\delta_{i,j}(t) := \mathbf{x}_i^G(t) - \mathbf{x}_j^O(t), \quad \bar{\delta}_{i,j}(T_k) := \frac{1}{|T_k|} \sum_{t \in T_k} \delta_{i,j}(t).$$

Then, we define the *center cost* $d_{i,j}(T_k)$ as the norm of the mean difference and the *shape cost* $s_{i,j}(T_k)$ as the average distance between frame-by-frame differences and the mean difference. Namely,

$$d_{i,j}(T_k) := \|\bar{\delta}_{i,j}(T_k)\|, \quad s_{i,j}(T_k) := \frac{1}{|T_k|} \sum_{t \in T_k} \|\delta_{i,j}(t) - \bar{\delta}_{i,j}(T_k)\|$$

with these two types of costs, the final assignment cost is calculated by

$$c_{i,j}(T_k) := d_{i,j}(T_k) + w \cdot s_{i,j}(T_k) \tag{1}$$

for a pre-defined shape weight $w > 1$.

As a result, each $\mathbf{x}_i^G(T_k)$ is matched with $\mathbf{x}_{\sigma_k(i)}^O(T_k)$ for $\sigma_k \in \mathrm{Sym}(m)$ (i.e., σ_k is a permutation of $\{1, \ldots, m\}$). That is, $\mathbf{x}_{\sigma_k(i)}^O(T_k)$ is expected to track the right player p_i in the video, and thus we can estimate the bias of $\mathbf{x}_i^G(T_k)$ by the mean difference from $\mathbf{x}_{\sigma_k(i)}^O(T_k)$.

Figure 3a shows an example of GPS-OTS trajectory matching in an anchor segment, where the red and blue curves indicate GPS and OTS trajectories, respectively. The circle at the end of each curve is the endpoint of the trajectory, and the number inside it is the player ID (i.e., the red and blue curves with the number i mean $\mathbf{x}_i^G(T_k)$ and $\mathbf{x}_i^G(T_k)$, respectively). The black arrow pointing to each of GPS trajectories $\mathbf{x}_i^G(T_k)$ indicates the estimated bias $\bar{\delta}_{i,\sigma(i)}(T_k)$, and the orange curve crossing the starting point of the arrow is the translated GPS trajectory (denoted as $\mathbf{x}_i^{G*}(T_k)$ in Sect. 3.4) by removing the bias from $\mathbf{x}_i^G(T_k)$.

According to Fig. 3, each GPS trajectory is matched well with a nearby OTS trajectory with a similar shape. The translated GPS trajectory is very close to its OTS counterpart, showing movement more physically natural. Especially, it seems that there is an ID switch between p_5 and p_8 in Sect. 3.1, but we correct it in this step by matching $\mathbf{x}_5^G(a_k)$ and $\mathbf{x}_8^O(a_k)$ and vice versa.

3.4　Initial Estimation of GPS Biases

Consequently, we can estimate a player's GPS bias per anchor segment by the mean difference between the matched pair of GPS and OTS trajectories. Moreover, we further approximate biases in non-anchor frames by linearly interpolating the estimated biases between neighboring anchor segments. In other words, we estimate GPS bias $\delta_i : \mathcal{T} \to \mathbb{R}^2$ of p_i on the total playing time $\mathcal{T}$ by

$$\delta_i(t) := \begin{cases} \bar{\delta}_{i,\sigma_k(i)}(T_k) & \text{if } a_k \leq t \leq b_k, 1 \leq k \leq K, \\ \delta_i(a_0) & \text{if } t < a_0, \\ \delta_i(b_K) & \text{if } t > b_K, \\ \dfrac{a_{k+1} - t}{a_{k+1} - b_k} \delta_i(b_k) + \dfrac{t - b_k}{a_{k+1} - b_k} \delta_i(a_{k+1}) & \text{if } b_k < t < a_{k+1}, 1 \leq k \leq K - 1. \end{cases}$$

for anchor segments $T_k = [a_k, b_k], 1 \leq k \leq K$.

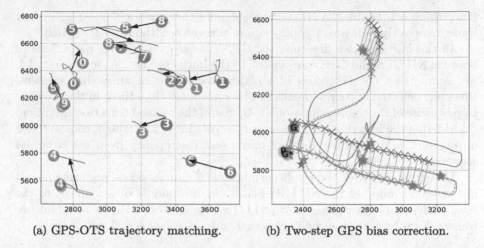

(a) GPS-OTS trajectory matching.   (b) Two-step GPS bias correction.

Fig. 3. Examples of GPS-OTS trajectory matching in an anchor segment and GPS bias correction in an interval including two anchor segments.

Removing these biases from GPS trajectories, we get a naive unbiased GPS (NU-GPS) trajectory

$$\mathbf{x}_i^{G*}(t) := \mathbf{x}_i^{G}(t) - \delta_i(t) \tag{2}$$

per player p_i as an intermediate product of our hybrid tracking.

3.5   Fine-Tuning GPS Biases

A drawback of NU-GPS trajectories is that intervals between adjoining anchor segments may not be short enough to ensure the accuracy of interpolated GPS biases in non-anchor frames. This sparsity of the anchor segment is attributed to the strict condition that every trajectory must have no spike in an anchor segment. Thus, we detect player-wise anchor frames using NU-GPS and bbox coordinates to shorten the length of the interval to be interpolated.

To be specific, we assign the bboxes $X^B(t) = \{\mathbf{x}_1^B(t), \ldots, \mathbf{x}_{m_t}^B(t)\}$ to the NU-GPS points $X^{G*}(t) = \{\mathbf{x}_1^{G*}(t), \ldots, \mathbf{x}_n^{G*}(t)\}$ by applying Hungarian algorithm again. As a result, some of $\mathbf{x}_i^{G*}(t)$ are matched with new OTS coordinates $\mathbf{x}_i^{O*}(t) \in X^B(t)$ where $\mathbf{x}_i^{O*}(t) \neq \mathbf{x}_j^{O*}(t)$ if $i \neq j$. Then, we regard t as player p_i's anchor frame if

(i)   every player's NU-GPS coordinate is matched with a bbox, i.e., $m_t \geq n$,
(ii) the maximum assignment cost among the matched pairs is less than or equal to a threshold value c_2,
(iii) the previous frame $t - \Delta t$ satisfies (i) and (ii), and
(iv) $\mathbf{x}_i^{O*}(t)$ is at physically reasonable distance from $\mathbf{x}_i^{O*}(t - \Delta t)$, i.e.,

$$v_i^{O*}(t) := \left\| \frac{\mathbf{x}_i^{O*}(t) - \mathbf{x}_i^{O*}(t - \Delta t)}{\Delta t} \right\| \leq v_0.$$

Since there is little bias in NU-GPS, we expect that each $\mathbf{x}_i^{O*}(t)$ at an anchor frame t correctly indicates the player p_i in the video without an ID switch.

As the last step, we fine-tune the GPS bias sequence using the difference between NU-GPS and OTS coordinates. In the initial prediction step in Sect. 3.4, we assume that the GPS bias of a player is constant in an anchor segment. However, detected anchor segments can be way longer than those in the previous step because of the unbiasedness of NU-GPS and the relaxed detection condition. Considering the fact that GPS biases vary across time, assuming a constant bias during such a long anchor segment may cause discrepancy from the true bias sequence.

Therefore, we divide the whole playing time $\mathcal{T}$ into λ-second segments ($\lambda = 4$ in our study) and set the NU-GPS bias δ_i^* in the middle of a segment to the mean difference between NU-GPS and OTS coordinates at the included anchor frames. Namely, for a λ-second segment $T = [t_0 - \frac{\lambda}{2}\,\mathrm{s}, t_0 + \frac{\lambda}{2}\,\mathrm{s})$, we assign

$$\delta_i^*(t_0) := \frac{1}{m} \sum_{t \in T \cap \mathcal{A}_i} \left(\mathbf{x}_i^{G*}(t) - \mathbf{x}_i^{O*}(t) \right)$$

where $\mathcal{A}_i$ is the set of p_i's anchor frames. We do not perform this step for segments in which less than half of the frames are anchors, and the biases in the middle remain undefined to be interpolated later.

In other words, we define the NU-GPS bias sequence $\delta_i^* : \mathcal{T} \to \mathbb{R}^2$ of $\mathbf{x}_i^{G*}$ at periodic base frames $c_1^i, \ldots, c_{K_i}^i \in \mathcal{T}$ where time differences between base frames are multiples of λ seconds. The δ_i^* at the remaining frames are defined by linear interpolation as in Sect. 3.4. Finally, we make the final prediction $\hat{\mathbf{y}}_i : \mathcal{T} \to \mathbb{R}^2$ of p_i's trajectory by removing the bias from the NU-GPS coordinates as follows:

$$\hat{\mathbf{y}}_i(t) := \mathbf{x}_i^{G*}(t) - \delta_i^*(t) = \mathbf{x}_i^G(t) - \delta_i(t) - \delta_i^*(t). \qquad (3)$$

Figure 3b depicts the two-step bias correction with a triple of GPS (red), NU-GPS (orange, dashed), and predicted (green) trajectories in a time interval. The $\times$ markers in GPS and NU-GPS trajectories correspond to the frames in anchor segments, so there is a constant difference plotted as parallel orange lines between pairs of GPS and NU-GPS coordinates in the same anchor segment. The long gap (i.e., red or orange curves without markers) between the two adjoining anchor segments give rise to the potential inaccuracy of linearly interpolated bias. Therefore, we assign bboxes to the dashed orange curve and compute the mean of frame-by-frame differences per λ-second segment with $\lambda = 4$. These segment-wise mean biases are assigned to the frames of orange $\star$ markers in NU-GPS trajectories, where removing them results in green $\star$ markers. The predicted trajectory is obtained by removing the interpolated bias from the NU-GPS trajectory. Note that the maximum length of interpolated intervals in the green trajectory (i.e., the maximum gap between adjacent $\star$'s) is much shorter than that in the orange trajectory (i.e., the maximum gap between adjacent $\times$'s).

4   Experiments

4.1   Data Preparation

Due to the difficulty of obtaining the ground truth data, we performed the hyper-parameter optimization and model evaluation tasks below on the same experimental dataset. The dataset has been acquired from a 15-min 5v5 possession game in soccer that simulated a session in FIFA Quality Test[1] 2022. We attached wearable GPS devices to players' upper back area and recorded the pitch by a fixed camera in 25 FPS at the same time. The raw 10 Hz GPS data with latitudes and longitudes were transformed into the local 2D coordinates relative to the pitch. In addition, we detected players in the video by fine-tuned YOLOv5 [9], after correcting the camera lens distortion using checkerboard calibration [27]. Assumed to be the bottom center of the detected bboxes, 2D coordinates in the video were also converted to the 2D pitch coordinates by homography transformation. Lastly, we synchronize the frequencies of GPS and bbox coordinates by down-sampling to 5 Hz (i.e., $\Delta t = 0.2$ s), the greatest common divisor of the frequencies of the two systems.

4.2   Implementation Detail

Using the above dataset, we have found the best combination of the hyperparameters by grid search. In Sect. 3.1, we set the threshold distance d_0 in (ii) and the threshold cost c_0 in (iii) to 0.75 m and 2.5 m, respectively. Among the total of 4,465 frames (893.0 s), 375 frames are detected as anchor starters.

For the coordinate matching between adjacent frames in Sect. 3.2, we set the threshold cost c_1 to 5.0 m/s $\cdot$ 0.2 s = 1.0 m, considering that higher speeds than 5.0 m/s can come from either actual sprints or inaccurate object detection. As a result, 40 anchor starters of the above 375 become the starting frames of valid anchor segments. The total duration of these 40 anchor segments is 154.2 s, accounting for 17.3% of the total playing time.

In Sect. 3.3, small w implies a strong influence of center cost, leaving the GPS-OTS trajectory matching not robust against a large GPS bias. On the contrary, large w weakens the effect of center cost, making the correct GPS trajectories hard to be distinguished from others with similar shapes. With these in mind, we choose $w = 5.0$.

In Sect. 3.5, we set $v_0 = 5.0$ m/s by the same reason for c_1 above. Meanwhile, we use $c_2 = 2.0$ m for player-wise anchor frame detection, which is smaller than $c_0 = 2.5$ m for anchor starter detection in Sect. 3.1. This is because bboxes are closer to NU-GPS coordinates rather than to GPS ones. In the last segment division, setting $\lambda = 4$ achieves the best performance in accuracy.

---

[1] https://www.fifa.com/technical/football-technology/standards/epts/epts-testing-process.

Table 1. Distance errors in centimeters per type of trajectories, and the proportion of data points within given each threshold distance from GT coordinates.

Type	Mean	Max	< 20 cm	< 30 cm	< 50 cm	< 100 cm
GPS	153.05	349.66	0.77%	1.61%	3.95%	16.10%
NU-GPS	26.33	182.50	47.45%	67.73%	88.08%	99.14%
Prediction	**17.72**	**177.71**	**69.32%**	**84.30%**	**95.45%**	**99.75%**

4.3 Model Evaluation

For the evaluation of our model, we compare a set of trajectories with the ground truth trajectories manually obtained in 5Hz by (1) correcting the ID switches and (2) fine-tuning the bbox locations. Namely, we regard a set $X(\mathcal{T}) = \{\mathbf{x}_1(\mathcal{T}), \ldots, \mathbf{x}_n(\mathcal{T})\}$ of player trajectories as accurate if the mean distance

$$e(X) := \frac{1}{n}\frac{1}{|\mathcal{T}|} \sum_{i=1}^{n} \sum_{t \in \mathcal{T}} \|\mathbf{x}_i(t) - \mathbf{y}_i(t)\| \qquad (4)$$

from the ground truth $Y = \{\mathbf{y}_1(\mathcal{T}), \ldots, \mathbf{y}_n(\mathcal{T})\}$ is small.

Table 1 compares the accuracies of raw GPS trajectories $X^G(\mathcal{T})$, NU-GPS trajectories $X^{G*}(\mathcal{T})$ resulting from Sect. 3.4, and the final predictions $\hat{Y}(\mathcal{T})$ from Sect. 3.5. We find that by our GPS-OTS hybrid tracking, the mean GPS distance error decreases from 153.04 cm to 17.72 cm. Also, we computed the maximum distance between each type of trajectory and the ground truth, which reduces from 349.66 cm to 177.71 cm. It is notable that 95.45% of predicted coordinates belong to the target circle of radius 50 cm, and almost 70% among them have errors closer than 20 cm. Regarding the width of a human body being about 50 cm, our results demonstrate an accuracy high enough for detailed multi-agent analysis.

5 Conclusion and Future Work

To our knowledge, this is the first approach that integrates GPS and OTS for player tracking. Automatically tracking multiple players at the same time without positional bias and ID switches, the proposed algorithm is shown to overcome the respective disadvantages of GPS and OTS at once.

However, we also leave several limitations for future work. Although the main tracking algorithm is fully automated, there remain manual steps in our framework, such as homography detection and GPS-video time synchronization. Moreover, this study only uses data from a single 15-min 5v5 session for both the hyperparameter tuning and model evaluation. Therefore, our method needs additional validation with a separate hold-out dataset, especially for another type of session such as regular 11v11 games.

By acquiring rich experimental data from various settings and adapting the algorithm using these data, we aim to make our method generally applicable to every possible condition including different types of sports games. Applying deep learning to some parts, such as anchor detection or trajectory interpolation, may enhance the performance and expandability of our framework.

References

1. Akyildiz, Z., Alvurdu, S., Ceylan, H.I., Clemente, F.M.: Validity and reliability of 10 Hz GPS sensor for measuring distance and maximal speed in soccer: Possible differences of unit positioning. In: Proceedings of the Institution of Mechanical Engineers, Part P: Journal of Sports Engineering and Technology (2022)
2. Bastida Castillo, A., Gómez Carmona, C.D., De la Cruz Sánchez, E., Pino Ortega, J.: Accuracy, intra- and inter-unit reliability, and comparison between GPS and UWB-based position-tracking systems used for time-motion analyses in soccer. Eur. J. Sport Sci. **18**(4), 450–457 (2018)
3. Bialkowski, A., Lucey, P., Carr, P., Yue, Y., Sridharan, S., Matthews, I.: Large-scale analysis of soccer matches using spatiotemporal tracking data. In: IEEE International Conference on Data Mining (2014)
4. Buchheit, M., Allen, A., Poon, T.K., Modonutti, M., Gregson, W., Salvo, V.D.: Integrating different tracking systems in football: multiple camera semi-automatic system, local position measurement and GPS technologies. J. Sports Sci. **32**(20), 1844–1857 (2014)
5. Fernández, J., Bornn, L.: Wide Open Spaces: A statistical technique for measuring space creation in professional soccer. In: MIT Sloan Sports Analytics Conference (2018)
6. Gadde, C.A., Jawahar, C.V.: Transductive weakly-supervised player detection using soccer broadcast videos. In: IEEE/CVF Winter Conference on Applications of Computer Vision (2022)
7. Hennessy, L., Jeffreys, I.: The current use of GPS, its potential, and limitations in soccer. Strength Cond. J. **40**(3), 83–94 (2018)
8. Hurault, S., Ballester, C., Haro, G.: Self-supervised small soccer player detection and tracking. In: ACM International Workshop on Multimedia Content Analysis in Sports, pp. 9–18 (2020)
9. Jocher, G., et al.: ultralytics/yolov5: v6.1 - TensorRT, TensorFlow Edge TPU and OpenVINO export and inference (2022)
10. Kim, H., Kim, B., Chung, D., Yoon, J., Ko, S.K.: SoccerCPD: Formation and role change-point detection in soccer matches using spatiotemporal tracking data. In: ACM SIGKDD International Conference on Knowledge Discovery and Data Mining (2022)
11. Kim, H., Kim, J., Chung, D., Lee, J., Yoon, J., Ko, S.K.: 6MapNet: representing soccer players from tracking data by a triplet network. In: ECML PKDD Workshop on Machine Learning and Data Mining for Sports Analytics (2021)
12. Komorowski, J., Kurzejamski, G., Sarwas, G.: FootandBall: integrated player and ball detector. In: International Joint Conference on Computer Vision, Imaging and Computer Graphics Theory and Applications (2020)
13. Kuhn, H.W.: The Hungarian method for the assignment problem. Nav. Res. Logist. Q. **2**(1–2), 83–97 (1955)

14. Linke, D., Link, D., Lames, M.: Validation of electronic performance and tracking systems EPTS under field conditions. PLoS ONE **13**(7), 1–19 (2018)
15. Malone, J.J., Lovell, R., Varley, M.C., Coutts, A.J.: Unpacking the black box: applications and considerations for using GPS devices in sport. Int. J. Sports Physiol. Perform. **12**, 18–26 (2017)
16. Naik, B.T., Hashmi, M.F., Geem, Z.W., Bokde, N.D.: DeepPlayer-Track: player and referee tracking with jersey color recognition in soccer. IEEE Access **10**, 32494–32509 (2022)
17. Pons, E., et al.: A comparison of a GPS device and a multi-camera video technology during official soccer matches: agreement between systems. PLoS ONE **14**(8), 1–12 (2019)
18. Pons, E., et al.: Integrating video tracking and GPS to quantify accelerations and decelerations in elite soccer. Sci. Rep. **11**(1), 18531 (2021)
19. Rossi, A., Pappalardo, L., Cintia, P., Fernández, J., Iaia, M.F., Medina, D.: Who is going to get hurt? predicting injuries in professional soccer. In: ECML PKDD Workshop on Machine Learning and Data Mining for Sports Analytics (2017)
20. Rossi, A., Pappalardo, L., Cintia, P., Iaia, F.M., Fernández, J., Medina, D.: Effective injury forecasting in soccer with GPS training data and machine learning. PLoS ONE **13**(7), 1–15 (2018)
21. Shaw, L., Glickman, M.: Dynamic analysis of team strategy in professional football. In: Barça Sport Analytics Summit (2019)
22. Spearman, W.: Beyond expected goals. In: MIT Sloan Sports Analytics Conference (2018)
23. Spearman, W., Basye, A., Dick, G., Hotovy, R., Pop, P.: Physics-based modeling of pass probabilities in soccer. In: MIT Sloan Sports Analytics Conference (2017)
24. Theagarajan, R., Bhanu, B.: An automated system for generating tactical performance statistics for individual soccer players from videos. IEEE Trans. Circuits Syst. Video Technol. **31**(2), 632–646 (2021)
25. Theiner, J., Gritz, W., Muller-Budack, E., Rein, R., Memmert, D., Ewerth, R.: Extraction of positional player data from broadcast soccer videos. In: IEEE/CVF Winter Conference on Applications of Computer Vision (2022)
26. Vandeghen, R., Cioppa, A., Van Droogenbroeck, M.: Semi-supervised training to improve player and ball detection in soccer. In: IEEE/CVF Conference on Computer Vision and Pattern Recognition (2022)
27. Zhang, Z.: A flexible new technique for camera calibration. IEEE Trans. Pattern Anal. Mach. Intell. **22**(11), 1330–1334 (2000)

Racket Sports

Predicting Tennis Serve Directions
with Machine Learning

Ying Zhu[✉] and Ruthuparna Naikar

Georgia State University, Atlanta, USA
yzhu@gsu.edu, rnaikar1@student.gsu.edu

Abstract. Serves, especially first serves, are very important in professional tennis. Servers choose their serve directions strategically to maximize their winning chances while trying to be unpredictable. On the other hand, returners try to predict serve directions to make good returns. The mind game between servers and returners is an important part of decision-making in professional tennis matches. To help understand the players' serve decisions, we have developed a machine learning method for predicting professional tennis players' first serve directions. Through feature engineering, our method achieves an average prediction accuracy of around 49% for male players and 44% for female players. Our analysis provides some evidence that top professional players use a mixed-strategy model in serving decisions and that fatigue might be a factor in choosing serve directions. Our analysis also suggests that contextual information is perhaps more important for returners' anticipatory reactions than previously thought.

Keywords: Tennis serve directions · Machine learning · Prediction

1 Introduction

At the beginning of each point in a tennis match, the serving player needs to decide where to direct the serve. There are three serve directions: wide, body (to the returner), and down-the-T (to the middle of the court) for each serve. Each player makes about 100 such decisions in a typical professional tennis match. These are important decisions because serves, especially first serves, are crucial in professional tennis matches [10, 12, 14]. A fast and well-placed first serve gives the server a big advantage. For example, based on ATP statistics [2], Novak Djokovic (world No. 1 for much of the last seven years) has won 76.5% of his first service points and 53.4% of his second service points. In other words, without his first serves, Djokovic was only slightly better than his opponents.

The player who serves (the server) chooses the serve directions strategically to maximize the winning chances. On the other hand, the player who returns the ball (the returner) will try to predict serve directions by analyzing serve patterns, which is especially important for the fast first serves. The average first serve speed is about 180 - 200 km/h for male tennis professionals and about 150 -

U. Brefeld et al. (Eds.): MLSA 2022, CCIS 1783, pp. 89–100, 2023.
https://doi.org/10.1007/978-3-031-27527-2_7

170 km/h for female professionals. With less than 0.5 s to react to such powerful serves, a returner needs a fast physical reaction and reasonably accurate anticipation. Previous research suggested that tennis players' anticipatory responses are informed by both the kinematics of serve motion and contextual information [18,19] but the nature of such anticipatory responses is still being debated [3].

The mind game between a server and a returner makes it an interesting case for studying human decision-making in a highly competitive environment. Some economists have used game theories to analyze professional players' serve patterns, with mixed results [1,4,5,16,21]. As more tennis data are available, Wei, et al. [22] have developed a machine learning method to predict serve directions by analyzing the Hawkeye data, with a prediction accuracy of 27.8%.

In this paper, we present our work on predicting professional tennis players' first serve directions by machine learning. Our machine learning model uses human annotated professional tennis match data, without video analysis or Hawkeye data. Through feature engineering and model tuning, we achieved an average prediction accuracy of about 49% for male players and about 44% for female players. Our results provide more insights into the behavior of both tennis servers and returners. Our analysis provides some evidence that top professional players use a mixed strategy for choosing serve directions and that fatigue might affect such decisions. In addition, our work shows that it is possible to achieve reasonable serve direction predictions solely based on contextual information, suggesting that contextual information is perhaps more important for returners' anticipatory reactions than previously thought.

Professional tennis players rarely reveal their on-court decision-making process. Since many decisions are made intuitively, a player may not even be aware of their own tendencies and patterns. Building machine learning models to predict serve directions may help us gain insights into their decision-making process as well as the differences between players.

Players and coaches may also use the machine learning model to evaluate the predictability of their serves. Our study shows that some players' serves are more predictable than others. Some players may be more predictable serving from the ad side than from the deuce side and vice versa. Such information can guide players to fine-tune their own games or study their opponents' games.

2   Related Work

Tennis data have been used in many academic research projects. Here we focus on the analysis of tennis serve directions. Some economists have used game theories to study the optimal strategy for choosing the serve directions. Walker and Wooder [21] analyzed ten professional tennis matches and found that the theory of mixed-strategy Nash equilibrium can largely explain the top players' selection of serve directions. They noted that top players tended to switch strategies frequently, resulting in serial dependence and higher predictability. Hsu, et al. [5] revisited Walker and Wooder's work using a broader data set and found no significant evidence of serial dependence. However, Spiliopoulos [16] analyzed the data from the Match Charting Project [15] and found some top male players had higher serial dependencies in serve directions than others. More recently, Gauriot, et al. [4] analyzed the Hawkeye data from over 3000 tennis matches played at the Australian Open and confirmed the finding by Walker and Wooder [21]. However, Anderson, et al. [1] analyzed the data from the Match Charting project [15] and rejected a key implication of a mixed-strategy Nash equilibrium, that the probability of winning a service game is the same for all serve directions. They argued that the dynamic programming strategy is more efficient than the mixed strategy.

Wei, et al. [22] analyzed the Hawkeye data from three years of the Australian Open men's draw and developed a method to predict serve directions. They considered 14 serve directions (seven for the deuce side and seven for the ad side) and used machine learning techniques (e.g., Random Forest) to make predictions. Their input parameters are score, player style, and opponent style. A player's style is the distribution of the player's serve count in the 14 directions. Their highest prediction accuracy is 27.8%.

Our work is similar to Wei, et al. [22] in that we both try to predict tennis serve directions using machine learning techniques. The difference is that we use the Match Charting Project data [15] instead of the Hawkeye data. We use a different set of features, and we adopt the commonly used six serve directions (wide, body, and down-the-T for the deuce or ad side) rather than 14 directions.

Kovalchik and Reid [7] analyzed the Hawkeye data from singles matches at the 2015 to 2017 Australian Open and built a taxonomy of shots via clustering. They reported the overall distributions of serve directions for the deuce and ad side separately but did not predict serve directions for individual players.

Tea and Swartz [17] analyzed the ball tracking data from the 2019 and 2020 Roland Garros tournaments, which contain 82 men's and 81 women's matches. They used Bayesian Multinomial Logistic Regression to build a predictive model of serve directions. They found discernible differences between male and female players and between individual players. Their model can output predictive distributions of serve directions. An example with Roger Federer's data was discussed, but the model prediction accuracy for individual players was not reported.

Whiteside and Reid [23] used machine learning (k-means clustering) to analyze the Hawkeye data of tennis serves to study the optimal landing locations for aces. They found three key elements related to serve aces: direction relative to the returner, closeness to the lines, and speed. De Leeuw, et al. [8] used subgroup discovery to find the characteristics of won service points for a specific professional tennis player. They found that more points were won if the player avoided hitting a backhand after the serve. These two studies are not relevant to our work on predicting serve directions.

Now we will look at serves from a returner's perspective. Returning first serves in professional tennis is one of the most difficult tasks in sports, and yet professional players have been able to return most first serves. Many analysts do not believe that fast physical reaction alone is enough to explain the many successful returns because the reaction time is less than 0.5 s. These players must have learned to read the serves with reasonable accuracy. However, the exact nature of this anticipatory behavior is still unknown [3]. The most widely examined source of anticipatory information has been the kinematics of serve motion. In other words, a returner might be able to predict the serve directions from reading the serve motion before the ball is hit. But professional players are trained to disguise their serve directions by maintaining the same serve motion. Therefore, reading the kinematics of serve motion is difficult. Some studies showed that contextual information might be useful for predicting the serve directions [18,19]. Our work is related to this subject because our results suggest that it is possible to make reasonably accurate predictions solely based on contextual information.

3 Basic Information About Tennis Serves

A tennis match is divided into sets, games, and points. A tennis court is laterally divided into two sides: the deuce side and the ad side. The two players take turns serving for each game. The serving player serves from the deuce side and ad side alternatively.

At the start of each point, the serving player has two chances to serve. If the first serve fails, the player can make a second serve. A player usually makes a faster but more risky first serve and a slower but safer second serve. The player can serve toward anywhere in the service box, but there are generally three directions: wide, body (toward the returner), and down-the-T (toward the middle of the court). In this study, we only consider the first serves because the first serves give the server a significant advantage. Therefore, in the discussions below, the word "serve" means "first serve" by default.

4 Data

We used the data from the Match Charting Project [15]. This open-source project provides detailed point-by-point and shot-by-shot data for thousands of professional tennis matches. Unlike the Hawkeye data, this data set is created by a group of volunteers watching tennis match videos and manually entering coded shot-by-shot data, including the serve directions and outcomes. An Excel script then derives additional information from the shot-by-shot data, such as the score, who is serving, and rally length for each point. The human-coded serve direction for each point is the ground truth for our model training and testing.

The data set we analyzed contains 3424 matches of 655 male players and 1916 matches of 422 female players. However, most players only have one or a few matches in the database. Therefore, we only run the analysis for a selected group of players with at least 30 matches.

We processed and analyzed the data using Python-based tools such as Pandas [9], Sklearn [13], SciPy [20], etc. The original data set contains errors, such as missing values in match data, duplicate or incorrect match IDs, match IDs in the point data set but are not in the match data set, and data entry errors in some shot-by-shot codes. So we spent a lot of time on data cleaning and transformation. The original data set primarily contains the scores and shot-by-shot descriptions for each match.

Several previous works [1,16] also used the Match Charting data, but they did not use machine learning.

5   Feature Engineering

The performance of a machine learning program depends on the selected features. We went through an iterative process of extracting, selecting, and testing features. In addition to the original features in the Match Charting data set, we also derived many new features from the original point-by-point and shot-by-shot data set. For example, we calculated the number of serves a player made toward each direction, identified critical points, calculated how many shots a player had played before each point, and estimated how much a player had run in the last point, etc.

Many features were tested and rejected. The features discussed in this paper are the ones that currently generate the highest prediction accuracy. We are still working on feature engineering. New features may be added, and some of the existing features may be modified or removed in the future.

We try to select features likely to influence a player's serve decisions. In addition to predicting serve directions, we also want to see if certain features are more important in making such decisions, which may help us gain insights into the players' decision-making process. We will discuss each of the selected features in the subsections below.

5.1   Outcome of Previous Points

We believe that the outcome of previous points would influence the selection of serve directions. We assume that a professional player would have a rough idea of how many points he or she has served toward each direction and how many points are won. This is the assumption made by several previous works [1,4,21]. The analysis by Spiliopoulos [16] also showed the serial dependency of serve directions on the previous point's serve direction and outcome.

The following features are calculated and used in our machine learning model.

– For each server and each point, our program calculates the count of the serves made toward each direction, from the beginning of the match to the previous point (3 features). These parameters are similar to the "prior style" parameters in Wei, et al. [22], but we only use three directions for the deuce or ad side while Wei, et al. used 7 directions for each side.

Although a player may not be able to remember the exact count of serves made toward each direction, the player should have a rough idea of the counts for the last several service games. Therefore, a variation of this feature is the counts of serve directions from a certain number of service games prior to the current point rather than from the beginning of the match. But it is not easy to determine how many prior service games should be considered.

- For each server and each point, our program also calculates the count of serves the server made toward each direction and won, from the beginning of the match to the previous point (3 features).

  Similarly, a variation of this feature is to count only for a certain number of service games before the current point, not from the beginning of the match. But it is not easy to determine how many prior service games should be considered.

- For each point, the program calculates the percentage of "good" first serves the server made toward each direction, from the beginning of the match to the previous point (3 features). These are the so-called "serve percentage" for each direction. A professional player should have a reasonably accurate understanding of their current serve percentage.

- For each point, the program record the winner of the previous point (1 feature).

5.2   Fatigue

As the match progresses, both players become more and more tired. We want to examine whether the level of fatigue is a factor in choosing serve directions. It is reasonable to assume that a player will exploit the opponent's fatigue in choosing serve directions. For example, serving wide is likely to make an opponent run more because a wide serve opens up the court more. The player's own fatigue may also affect serve directions. Because the net is lower in the middle, serving to the T may require less jumping.

The following features are used to estimate fatigue in our machine learning model.

- For each point, our program calculates the cumulative run indexes for two players from the beginning of the match to the previous point (2 features). They indicate how tired each player is from the running and hitting before each serve.

Because the Match Charting data [15] contains detailed shot-by-shot information, including the shot type (e.g., forehand, backhand, slice, volley, overhead), shot direction (i.e., to-deuce-side, to-middle, or to-ad-side), and the depth of each shot (e.g., shallow and deep), our program can infer the player's court position when they hit a particular shot. Based on that information, the program can estimate how much a player ran for each point and calculate a "run index." It is more accurate than the shot (rally) count because it includes running.

This run index is not as accurate as the Hawkeye data for measuring running distance, but it is a consistent estimate from point to point. Since Hawkeye data are not publicly available, it is difficult to get more accurate measures.

5.3   Performance Anxiety

Because a tennis match does not have a time limit, scoreboard pressure is the primary source of a player's performance anxiety. Such anxiety could influence a player's decisions. For this reason, Wei, et al. [22] used scores in their machine learning model. But our method is different. Instead of using scores, we calculate an index of each player's performance anxiety. Our work is based on the OCC model [11] of emotion, which is the standard model in affective computing. Based on the OCC model, anxiety is influenced by hope, fear, and uncertainty.

A player's feeling of uncertainty is related to the gap between the two players' scores. The smaller the gap, the higher the uncertainty. If the score is tied, the uncertainty is the highest. If one player is very close to winning, the uncertainty is very low. Due to tennis' hierarchical score structure, there are three levels of uncertainty. The gap between the set scores influences the match-level uncertainty. The gap between the game scores influences the set-level uncertainty. The gap between the point scores influences the game-level uncertainty.

A player's feeling of hope depends on how close the player is to winning. If a player's score is close to the winning score, the player's hope is high. Again, there are three levels of hope: match-level hope, set-level hope, and game-level hope.

A player's feeling of fear depends on how close the player is to losing. There are three levels of fear: match-level fear, set-level fear, and game-level fear.

For example, if a player leads by a significant margin and serves for the set point, the player's hope is high, fear is low, and uncertainty is low, resulting in a relatively low level of anxiety. On the other hand, if the scores are very close near the end of a match, such as in the final set tiebreak, each player will have high hope, high fear, and high uncertainty, resulting in high levels of anxiety for both players.

In our model, a performance anxiety index is calculated separately on the game, set, and match level based on the following equation (3 features).

$$performance\_anxiety = uncertainty * (hope + fear)$$

The overall performance anxiety is the sum of game, set, and match level anxiety indices (1 feature).

$$overall\_anxiety = game\_anxiety + set\_anxiety + match\_anxiety$$

In the equation, we do not consider fear to be the negative of hope. Therefore, fear does not reduce hope, and vice versa. This is because hope and strong coexist in most situations. For example, in a close tiebreak game, a player is close to both victory and defeat at the same time. In such cases, both strong hope and strong fear can coexist.

5.4   Other Features

We also considered other factors that may influence the serve decisions, such as court surfaces [6] and the opponent's handedness. For example, a player might serve differently against a lefty opponent.

6   Machine Learning

We ranked the players by the number of matches they have in the data set and analyzed players with at least 30 matches in the data set. Due to the space limit, we only present the results for ten male players and ten female players. The players are selected based on their current ranking and significant achievements. But the results for other players are generally consistent with those presented here.

We applied the following machine learning models to our data set: Multinomial Logistic Regression, Decision Tree, Random Forest, Support Vector Machine (Multiclass Classification), and Neural Network. We also applied Bagging classifier, Ada Boost classifier, and XGBoost classifier, but the results are no better than the models mentioned above, so we do not present their results here.

For Random Forest, we used 200 trees with a maximum depth of 150. For the Bagging classifier, we used 50 estimators. For the Ada Boost classifier, we used 70 estimators. For the XGBoost classifier, the K value is 10. For the neural network, we use sklearn.neural_network.MLPClassifier() with two hidden layers (200, 100).

We train our models individually for each selected player. For each player, we randomly split the data into a training set (70%) and a testing set (30%), and we use the same training set and testing sets for the different machine learning models. For each player, our program selects all the points that this player serves, and predicts the first serve direction using the features discussed in Sect. 5. The prediction is then compared with the actual first serve direction coded by the person who entered the data for the Match Charting project. The prediction accuracy is calculated based on all the points in the testing data set.

The results of the analysis are presented in Tables 1, 2, 3, and 4. In the tables, LR stands for Multinomial Logical Regression, DT stands for decision tree, RF stands for Random Forest, SVM stands for Support Vector Machine, and NN stands for Neural Network.

Table 1. First Serve Direction Prediction Accuracy for the Deuce Side Serves (men)

First name	Last name	LR	RF	DT	SVM	NN	MEAN
Novak	Djokovic	0.47	0.50	0.45	0.46	0.47	0.47
Roger	Federer	0.46	0.49	0.44	0.47	0.47	0.47
Nick	Kyrgios	0.55	0.52	0.50	0.55	0.54	0.53
Daniil	Medvedev	0.45	0.49	0.48	0.47	0.46	0.47
Andy	Murray	0.56	0.53	0.58	0.52	0.54	0.55
Rafael	Nadal	0.52	0.50	0.43	0.52	0.52	0.50
Dominic	Thiem	0.55	0.47	0.43	0.55	0.55	0.51
Stefanos	Tsitsipas	0.49	0.48	0.46	0.47	0.47	0.47
Stan	Wawrinka	0.46	0.49	0.45	0.45	0.48	0.46
Alexander	Zverev	0.46	0.42	0.42	0.47	0.46	0.44
	MEAN	0.50	0.49	0.46	0.49	0.50	0.49

Table 2. First Serve Direction Prediction Accuracy for the Ad Side Serves (men)

First name	Last name	LR	RF	DT	SVM	NN	MEAN
Novak	Djokovic	0.49	0.50	0.44	0.49	0.48	0.48
Roger	Federer	0.56	0.52	0.53	0.59	0.56	0.55
Nick	Kyrgios	0.50	0.49	0.45	0.48	0.48	0.48
Daniil	Medvedev	0.53	0.51	0.53	0.49	0.60	0.53
Andy	Murray	0.48	0.45	0.44	0.48	0.47	0.46
Rafael	Nadal	0.54	0.51	0.45	0.54	0.54	0.52
Dominic	Thiem	0.58	0.54	0.52	0.58	0.58	0.56
Stefanos	Tsitsipas	0.47	0.45	0.42	0.48	0.47	0.46
Stan	Wawrinka	0.49	0.49	0.43	0.49	0.47	0.47
Alexander	Zverev	0.45	0.47	0.44	0.44	0.44	0.45
	MEAN	0.51	0.49	0.47	0.51	0.51	0.50

Table 3. First Serve Direction Prediction Accuracy for the Deuce Side Serves (women)

First name	Last name	LR	RF	DT	SVM	NN	MEAN
Victoria	Azarenka	0.47	0.47	0.40	0.49	0.48	0.46
Ashleigh	Barty	0.51	0.45	0.45	0.51	0.48	0.48
Angelique	Kerber	0.37	0.37	0.33	0.40	0.36	0.36
Anett	Kontaveit	0.41	0.43	0.39	0.39	0.39	0.40
Garbine	Muguruza	0.47	0.45	0.40	0.47	0.45	0.45
Naomi	Osaka	0.49	0.41	0.41	0.48	0.45	0.45
Karolina	Pliskova	0.44	0.45	0.40	0.43	0.44	0.43
Maria	Sakkari	0.44	0.44	0.37	0.47	0.47	0.44
Iga	Swiatek	0.41	0.43	0.36	0.43	0.44	0.41
Serena	Williams	0.48	0.49	0.44	0.49	0.49	0.48
	MEAN	0.45	0.44	0.40	0.46	0.45	0.44

We also calculated the serve direction distributions for each player. Our results are similar to those reported by Tea and Swartz [17]. The serve direction distributions vary from player to player. For example, Djokovic's serve directions are more evenly distributed, while Federer tended to serve much less to the body.

7   Discussion

From Tables 1 and 2, we can see that our machine learning models achieved an average 49% prediction accuracy for the deuce side serve directions and 50% accuracy for the ad side serve directions for the selected male players. Adding other male players will bring the average percentage slightly lower to around

Table 4. First Serve Direction Prediction Accuracy for the Ad Side Serves (women)

First name	Last name	LR	RF	DT	SVM	NN	MEAN
Victoria	Azarenka	0.46	0.41	0.34	0.47	0.43	0.42
Ashleigh	Barty	0.51	0.46	0.45	0.46	0.46	0.47
Angelique	Kerber	0.61	0.58	0.48	0.61	0.60	0.58
Anett	Kontaveit	0.43	0.42	0.42	0.43	0.42	0.42
Garbine	Muguruza	0.39	0.40	0.38	0.37	0.40	0.39
Naomi	Osaka	0.44	0.38	0.36	0.45	0.47	0.42
Karolina	Pliskova	0.43	0.42	0.42	0.46	0.44	0.43
Maria	Sakkari	0.50	0.51	0.45	0.50	0.53	0.50
Iga	Swiatek	0.49	0.40	0.37	0.49	0.43	0.44
Serena	Williams	0.47	0.47	0.45	0.47	0.48	0.47
	MEAN	0.47	0.44	0.41	0.47	0.47	0.45

48%. From Tables 3 and 4, we can see that our machine learning models achieved an average 44% prediction accuracy for the deuce side serve directions and 45% accuracy for the ad side serve directions for the selected female players. Adding other female players will bring the average percentage slightly lower to around 43%. From the tables, we can also see that prediction accuracy is generally consistent among different machine learning methods.

We found only one published work by Wei, et al. [22] that reported a serve direction prediction accuracy (27.8%). However, it is difficult to compare our prediction accuracy with theirs because Wei, et al. used seven serve directions per side while we used the more traditional three directions per side. This is because we based our analyses on different ground truths. Wei. et al. used the Hawkeye data as ground truth, and they could divide the serve directions into smaller groups. We used human-observed serve directions as our ground truth, and our data only has three serve directions per side. The features we used are also quite different from the features used by Wei, et al.

We conducted a feature importance analysis for the Decision Tree model. We found that the most important features are the cumulative counts of first serves made to each direction, the run index of the server in the previous point, and the first serve percentage for each direction. While the prediction accuracy varies for each player, these three features are consistently among the most important. This provides some indirect evidence that they might also be the important factors a player considers when choosing serve directions. The importance of cumulative counts of first serve directions and first serve percentage are consistent with the mixed-strategy findings by Walker and Wooder [21], Spiliopoulos [16], and Gauriot, et al. [4]. But as far as we know, the importance of server fatigue (run index) in choosing the serve direction has not been discussed in previous work.

Finally, our results show that it is possible to achieve reasonably accurate prediction of serve directions solely based on contextual information such as the outcome of previous serves, performance anxiety, and fatigue. This may help explain why professional players are able to return most of the very fast first serves. Many analysts do not believe that fast physical reaction alone is enough to explain the many successful first serve returns because a returner must react to a first serve in less than 0.5 s. These players must have learned to read the serves with reasonable accuracy. Although the exact nature of this anticipatory behavior is still unclear [3], the most widely examined source of anticipatory information has been the kinematics of serve motion. In other words, a returner might be able to predict the serve directions from reading the serve motion before the ball is hit. But professional players are trained to disguise their serve directions by maintaining the same serve motion, making it difficult to read. Some studies showed that contextual information might be useful for predicting the serve directions [18,19]. Our work suggests that contextual information is perhaps more important for returners' anticipatory reactions than previously thought.

8   Conclusion and Future Work

We have described our machine learning methods for predicting professional tennis players' first serve directions. Through feature engineering, our method achieves an average prediction accuracy of around 49% for male players and 44% for female players.

Our feature importance analysis provides some indirect evidence that the top professional players seem to use a mixed-strategy model in choosing serve directions, which is consistent with some previous works [4,16,21]. However, the importance of server fatigue in choosing the serve direction has been a new discovery. Our work also suggests that contextual information is perhaps more important for returners' anticipatory reactions than previously thought.

We are continuing our work on feature engineering to improve prediction accuracy. We will also test using Brier Score as a measurement of prediction accuracy. We also plan to apply our method to applications in other highly competitive situations.

References

1. Anderson, A., Rosen, J., Rust, J., Wong, K.P.: Disequilibrium play in tennis. Working papers, Georgetown University (2021). http://ideas.repec.org/p/geo/guwopa/gueconwpa~21-21-07.html
2. Association of Tennis Professionals (ATP): ATP Stats. http://www.atptour.com/en/stats
3. Avilés, C., Navia, J.A., Ruiz, L.M.: Óscar Martínez de Quel: do expert tennis players actually demonstrate anticipatory behavior when returning a first serve under representative conditions? a systematic review including quality assessment and methodological recommendations. Psychol. Sport Exerc. **43**, 16–26 (2019)
4. Gauriot, R., Page, L., Wooders, J.: Expertise, gender, and equilibrium play. Tech. rep., New York University Abu Dhabi, United Arab Emirates (2020). http://www.johnwooders.com/papers/Expertise,Gender,andEquilibrium.pdf

5. Hsu, S.H., Huang, C.Y., Tang, C.T.: Minimax play at Wimbledon: comment. Am. Econ. Rev. **97**, 517–523 (2007)
6. Hughes, M., Clarke, S.: Surface effect on elite tennis strategy. In: Reilly, T., Hughes, M., Lees, A. (eds.) Science and Racket Sports I, pp. 288–294. Taylor & Francis (2021)
7. Kovalchik, S., Reid, M.: A shot taxonomy in the era of tracking data in professional tennis. J. Sports Sci. **36**, 2096–2104 (2018)
8. de Leeuw, A.-W., Hoekstra, A., Meerhoff, L., Knobbe, A.: Tactical analyses in professional tennis. In: Cellier, P., Driessens, K. (eds.) ECML PKDD 2019. CCIS, vol. 1168, pp. 258–269. Springer, Cham (2020). https://doi.org/10.1007/978-3-030-43887-6_20
9. McKinney, W.: Data structures for statistical computing in python. In: Proceedings of the 9th Python in Science Conference, pp. 56–61 (2010)
10. Mecheri, S., Rioult, F., Mantel, B., Kauffmann, F., Benguigui, N.: The serve impact in tennis: first large-scale study of big hawk-eye data. Statist. Anal. Data Mining **9**, 310–325 (2016)
11. Ortony, A., Clore, G.L., Collins, A.: The cognitive structure of emotions. Cambridge University Press (1988)
12. O'Donoghue, G.P., Brown, E.: The importance of service in grand slam singles tennis. Int. J. Perform. Anal. Sport **8**, 70–78 (2017)
13. Pedregosa, F., et al.: Scikit-learn: machine learning in Python. J. Mach. Learn. Res. **12**, 2825–2830 (2011)
14. Rioult, F., Mecheri, S., Mantel, B., Kauffmann, F., Benguigui, N.: What can hawk-eye data reveal about serve performance in tennis? In: Proceedings of the Machine Learning and Data Mining for Sports Analytics workshop (ECML/PKDD), pp. 36–45 (2015)
15. Sackmann, J.: The match charting project. Available at http://www.tennisabstract.com/. Accessed 19 Jun 2022
16. Spiliopoulos, L.: Randomization and serial dependence in professional tennis matches: do strategic considerations, player rankings and match characteristics matter? Judgm. Decis. Mak. **13**, 413–427 (2016)
17. Tea, P., Swartz, T.B.: The analysis of serve decisions in tennis using Bayesian hierarchical models. Ann. Oper. Res. **2021**, 1–16 (2022)
18. Vernon, G.: Decision making in tennis: exploring the use of kinematic and contextual information during anticipatory performance, Ph. D. thesis, Victoria University, Australia (2020)
19. Vernon, G., Farrow, D., Reid, M.: Returning serve in tennis: a qualitative examination of the interaction of anticipatory information sources used by professional tennis players. Front. Psychol. **9**, 895 (2018)
20. Virtanen, P., et al.: SciPy 1.0: fundamental algorithms for scientific computing in python. Nat. Methods **17**, 261–272 (2020)
21. Walker, M., Wooders, J.: Minimax play at Wimbledon. Am. Econ. Rev. **91**(5), 1521–1538 (2001)
22. Wei, X., Lucey, P., Morgan, S., Carr, P., Reid, M., Sridharan, S.: Predicting serves in tennis using style priors. In: Proceedings of the 21th ACM SIGKDD International Conference on Knowledge Discovery and Data Mining, pp. 2207–2215. ACM (2015)
23. Whiteside, D., Reid, M.: Spatial characteristics of professional tennis serves with implications for serving aces: a machine learning approach. J. Sports Sci. **35**, 648–654 (2016)

Discovering and Visualizing Tactics in a Table Tennis Game Based on Subgroup Discovery

Pierre Duluard[1], Xinqing Li[2], Marc Plantevit[3], Céline Robardet[2(✉)], and Romain Vuillemot[1]

[1] Univ Lyon, Centrale Lyon, CNRS, INSA Lyon, UCBL, Univ Lyon 2, LIRIS, UMR5205, 69130 Ecully, France
[2] Univ Lyon, INSA Lyon, CNRS, UCBL, LIRIS, UMR5205, 69621 Villeurbanne, France
celine.robardet@insa-lyon.fr
[3] Laboratoire de Recherche de l'EPITA (LRE), Le Kremlin-Bicêtre, Paris 94276, France

Abstract. We report preliminary results to automatically identify effective tactics of elite table tennis players. We define these tactics as subgroups of winning strokes that table tennis experts seek to identify in order to train players and adapt their strategy during play. We first report how we identify and classify these subgroups using the weighted relative accuracy measure (WRAcc). We then present the subgroups using visualizations to communicate these results to our expert. These exchanges allow rapid feedback on our results and makes it possible further improvements to our discoveries.

Keywords: Data mining · Sports data visualization · Table tennis

1 Introduction

Table tennis is a racket sport ranked amongst the most popular physical activities played at both amateur and elite levels. It is practiced and followed by millions of sports enthusiasts, especially as an Olympic discipline since the Olympic Games of Seoul 1988. Thus, many international federations and clubs train players all around the world at various levels. Academics have also focused on this sport in many areas from video tracking to data mining and visualization. In this work we contribute to this area of research by reporting on a close collaboration with an organization in charge of training elite players, the **Table Tennis National partner (TTN)**[1]. This organization recently annotated videos of elite player games to evaluate descriptive game statistics (e.g., number of wins per type of serve). They sought to improve analysis of such datasets to train elite players and improve their tactical preparation before games. They also sought to get

---

[1] Anonymized.

U. Brefeld et al. (Eds.): MLSA 2022, CCIS 1783, pp. 101–112, 2023.
https://doi.org/10.1007/978-3-031-27527-2_8

such analysis during games to provide insights to players on which strategy to focus on.

The challenge in this work is to reveal hidden patterns from table tennis datasets which contain short, yet rich stroke sequences, grouped by rally. Table tennis games usually contain up to a hundred rallies composed of a series of (on average) half a dozen strokes each. Each rally ends with a score increased by one for one of the two players. Rallies are composed of multi-variate strokes with laterality (side of the racket being used), type of stroke and impact zone on the table. Many other parameters enter into account to analyze rallies such as who serves, players scores and previous sets won by each player.

Table tennis sport recently gained interest from data mining and visualization [7,9]. Two main contributions have been proposed to visualize tactics in racket sports. The iTTVis [9] offers an interactive visualization system that works for analyzing and exploring table tennis data. The system is divided into several parts, and each part presents the evolution of the match from a different aspect. It also summarizes the statistical correlation of inter and intra stroke attributes. In other words, it shows the relationships of attributes of each stroke and between strokes. It does, however, rely on expert visual analysis of each rally to identify tactical patterns. Tac-Miner [7] is more advanced on this point. It focuses more on tactics than on the match. By merging several matches into a single presentation, it allows the analysis of several matches against the same opponent. It presents a tactic either globally, using frequency and win rate, or precisely, using detailed attributes. Players and study attributes can be selected. Compared to iTTVis, it lacks integrity in the evolution of the whole match, but shows more comparative and correlation analysis of different tactics.

In a first approach, we performed an exploratory data analysis using simple statistics such as data distribution and frequency calculation. This gave us a good overview of the games. We also explored several synchronized views deployed for our partner as a dashboard to quickly explore data without technical expertise (Fig. 1). This approach allowed our experts to develop a deeper understanding of the tactical possibilities from the data. However, they did not identify complex tactics involving action sequences. After several weeks of discussions, we have identified the following issues to address regarding tactical analysis using sequences:

– What are the most effective serve and hit zone combinations?
– Are there recurring behaviors to win a rally?
– How to characterize player profiles?

These questions are so far under-explored by analysts or are resolved by subjective analysis. Recent research has focused on intra-stroke analysis whereas we aim to focus on the tactical level by exploring discriminant sub-sequences to identify tactics. In particular, we focus on winning stroke combinations to characterize the players' tactics. In the following, we also provide visual representations so that experts can quickly grasp the result and get context about the sequences.

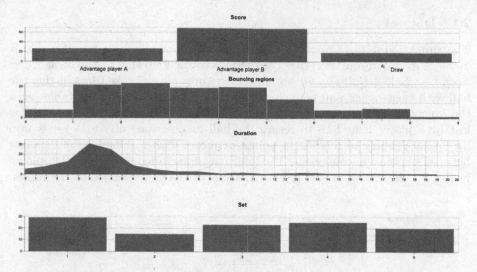

Fig. 1. Game statistics for a table tennis game between two players.

2   Methodology

The goal of our research is to discover useful tactics that lead to success. According to the **TTN**, a tactic consists of two consecutive strokes for a player, which means that a tactic consists of three consecutive strokes. Indeed, the player, who serves, perfectly controls the first two strokes of an exchange, which can thus constitute a tactic, while thereafter he acts according to the actions of his opponent. Finding useful tactics is not exclusive to table tennis competitions, but pertains to many other sports. We find a similar problem in an article on football [2], which addresses the problems of low repetition between items of a sequence and the inequality of sequence length. It uses Dynamic Time Wrapping (DTW) [6] to compute the similarity between two sequences of different length, then uses CM-SPADE [3] to find frequent sub-sequences. However, unlike soccer, table tennis data has close relationships between players and stroke order. In football games, we define a sequence as a list of consecutive moves within a limited time interval, which can include several continuous moves by the same player or moves by different players at the same time. In contrast, the sequences set in a table tennis match are actually a rally. Thus, in a list of consecutive moves, the two players appear alternately in the sequence, which implies a strong correspondence between the sequence of stocks and the player. The use of the DTW, which can associate items with different positions in the two sequences, causes in this situation problems of correspondence because we cannot say that a stoke of player A is similar to a stroke of player B in our situation. This is why we turn to the extraction of frequent and/or discriminating sub-strings. These concepts are formally presented below.

2.1   Dataset

The annotated dataset we work with comes from a single table tennis game. It includes match information that corresponds to the following hierarchical order: $Match \rightarrow Set \rightarrow Rally \rightarrow Stroke$. In table tennis, players take turns hitting the ball with their racket and bouncing it off the opponent's side of the table (with the exception of the serve, which must bounce off both sides). Thus, a rally is lost by a player if he fails to return the ball as described above. A set is won by a player when he reaches 11 points or more, with a difference of 2 points between him and his opponent. The information included at each level is shown in Fig. 2.   In this work, the level of analysis of the game relates to the rallies,

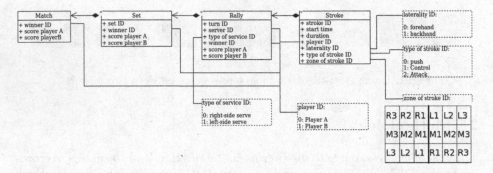

Fig. 2. Table tennis game data model. In this work we are mainly interested in stroke sequences whose attributes are described in table Stroke. Notice the locations of the 9 possible impact zones on the table.

that is to say the sequences of strokes until winning by one of the two players. Additional information provides context to the rallies, and we will use the score result as the criteria for success in such a rally (and possibly the tactics used in it). Notice that a sequence of strokes (i.e., a rally) has the following structure:

- It begins with a serve (Rss for a right side serve and Lss for a left side serve of a player) which hits an impact zone (9 possible areas Z1 to Z9, see Fig. 2) on the opponent's table part.
- There follows a sequence of strokes described by the type of stroke (C for a Control, A for an Attack and P for a Push), the laterality (B for a Backhand and F for a Forehand) and the hit zone (Z1 to Z9).

Those choices are justified in Sect. 2.4. It is possible to use a graph to represent a set of rallies, as shown in Fig. 3. The nodes of the graph represent the strokes and the edges represent the transitions between the strokes (the edges are then labeled with a number equal to the number of rallies concerned by the transition). We also order the nodes so that we read the rallies from left to right: the leftmost node is the serve and the rightmost node indicates the winner of the rally.

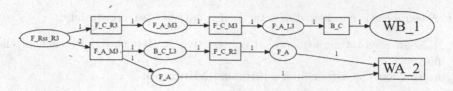

Fig. 3. Example of rally represented by a graph: each node is a stroke (player A is represented as squares, player B as circles).

The square nodes represent the strokes of Player A, while the oval ones represent the strokes of Player B.

For example, this graph represents three rallies. The first one is **Player A's Forehand Right side serve in R3** → **Player B's Forehand Attack in M3** → **Player A's Forehand Control in M3** → ... → **Player B wins**. The two other rallies begin similarly with **Player A's Forehand Right side serve in R3** → **Player B's Forehand Attack in M3** and are then different until **Player A** wins.

2.2 Tactics in Table Tennis

We define tactics as a sequence of consecutive strokes whose goal is to win the point for the player who uses it. According to **TTN**, a tactic can be seen as a sequence of three consecutive strokes even if the three strokes are not related to the same player. However, we assume the server perfectly controls his first two strokes of an exchange. Thus, with his service, he reduces the possible strokes of his opponent. This echoes previous work in tactical analysis [7,8]. A tactic occurs several times during the game and generalizes a sequence of strokes by identifying the key elements that characterize it (laterality, type or area).

2.3 Mining Frequent and Discriminant Sequential Pattern

Each such sequence is associated to a label that indicates the player who won the rally (WA if it is player A, WB otherwise). The set of such sequences is denoted $\mathcal{D}$ in the following.

From the sequences that represent rallies we consider subsequences that occur frequently in the data [3]. The occurrence of one sequence in another is specified in Definition 1.

Definition 1 (Occurrence of a sequence in another one). *A sequence $S_A = X_1, X_2, \cdots, X_k$, where $X_1, X_2, \cdots, X_k$ are itemsets, is said to occur in another sequence $S_B = Y_1, Y_2, \cdots, Y_m$, where $Y_1, Y_2, \cdots, Y_m$ are also itemsets, if and only if there exists integers $1 \le i_1 < i_2 < \cdots < i_k \le m$ such that $X_1 \subseteq Y_{i_1}$, $X_2 \subseteq Y_{i_2}$, ... $X_k \subseteq Y_{i_k}$. It is denoted by $S_A \sqsubseteq S_B$. The support of S_A in the database $\mathcal{D}$ is the number of sequences $S \in \mathcal{D}$ where $S_A \sqsubseteq S$ divided by the total number of sequences in $\mathcal{D}$.*

A sequence is considered as a tactic if it satisfies two constraints:

1. it is an alternating sequence of consecutive strokes played by each of the players,
2. its frequency is higher than a threshold **MinSupp**.

Definition 2 (Alternate sequence). *An sequence $S_A = X_1, \cdots, X_n$ is alternate if all the itemsets with an even index are played by a player, and the odd ones by the other player. Furthermore, the itemsets are consecutive in the sequences $S \in \mathcal{D}$ where S_A is considered to occur: considering $S = Y_1, \cdots, Y_m$, we have $S_A \sqsubseteq S$ if there exists an integer $1 < i < m - n + 1$ such that $X_1 \subseteq Y_i$, $X_2 \subseteq Y_{i+1}, \cdots, X_n \subseteq Y_{i+n-1}$.*

To be able to answer the question of interest of the **TTN**, we perform supervised descriptive rule discovery [4]. In our context, it consists in discovering alternate sequential patterns whose supporting rallies are mainly won by a given player j. This is what is called subgroup discovery [1]. The quality of an alternate sequence to describe the tactic of player j is measured by the Weighted Relative Accuracy measure (WRAcc) [5]. It requires defining a measure of support on player j's winning rallies, $\mathbf{Supp}(S, \mathcal{D}_j)$, as the number of sequences with label W_J where the sequence S occurs, divided by the total number of sequences with label W_J.

Definition 3 (Weighted relative accuracy). *Weighted relative accuracy of an alternate sequence S to characterize the winning rallies of player j is defined by*

$$WRAcc(S, W_j) = P(S) \cdot (P(W_j|S) - P(W_j))$$
$$= \mathbf{Supp}(S, \mathcal{D}) \cdot \left(\frac{\mathbf{Supp}(S, \mathcal{D}_j)}{\mathbf{Supp}(S, \mathcal{D})} - \mathbf{Supp}(\langle\rangle, \mathcal{D}_j) \right)$$

with $\langle\rangle$ the empty sequence that generalizes all the sequences of the dataset.

We use SPADE [3] to compute frequent alternate sequences. We adapt it by modifying the sequence containment used in the algorithm.

2.4   Summary of Assumptions

A first category of assumptions is related to the choices of possible values for each attribute when annotating a stroke. These choices were made by the **TTN**.

According to the **TTN**, for the types of strokes, the choice of the three values (attack, control and push) allows to describe the player's intention, which is for the **TTN** more important than knowing the exact technique used for the stroke.

Regarding the zones on the tennis table, the separation into 3 side zones (L, M and R) is enough to describe whether a ball is sent to the player, or to his forehand or his backhand. According to the **TTN** the separation into 3 depth zones (1, 2 and 3) is sufficient to describe the player's intention.

A second category of assumptions concerns how to define a tactic. Indeed, it was agreed with the **TTN** that a tactic would be an alternation by each player of three consecutive strokes. Indeed, the rallies are only composed of 3 to 4 strokes on average and it is therefore useless to be interested in longer tactics.

In addition, it was decided that all the tactics of a player in a winning rally were winning. This choice makes it easy to classify the tactics.

3   Results

We applied the methodology introduced in the previous section to a match that opposes elite players (**Player A** and **Player B**) during an international game. In order to effectively communicate our results with the **Table Tennis National partner**, we also designed several visualizations of table tennis sequences.

3.1   Presentation of the Obtained Alternate Sequences

In this part, we use the SPADE algorithm to determine the most frequent tactics (with **MinSupp**=5%) then we calculate the WRAcc measure for each of them in order to only keep the most relevant ones. The most interesting subgroups for each player are represented in Tables 1 and 2

Table 1. Player A's tactics extracting by SPADE with high WRAcc.

WRAcc	Frequency	Winrate	Player A's stroke	Player B's stroke	Player A's stroke
0.02984	12.9%	78.6%	M1	Forehand	Forehand
0.02984	12.9%	78.6%	M1	Forehand	Attack
0.02984	12.9%	78.6%	M1	Forehand, Push	Forehand
0.02984	12.9%	78.6%	M1	Forehand, Push	Attack
0.02881	14.8%	75.0%	M1	Push	Attack
0.02469	5.6%	100.0%	Right-side Serve	Forehand	R3

Table 2. Player B's tactics extracting by SPADE with high WRAcc.

WRAcc	Frequency	Winrate	Player B's stroke	Player A's stroke	Player B's stroke
0.03086	5.6%	100.0%	Forehand	Push	R3
0.02881	11.1%	66.7%	Forehand	Control	L3
0.02778	8.3%	77.8%	R3	Control	Forehand
0.02778	9.3%	70.0%	Forehand	Control	Attack, L3
0.02778	8.3%	77.8%	R3	Forehand, Control	Forehand
0.02675	19.4%	66.7%	Forehand	Control	Attack

The previous tactics are calculated on the complete dataset, thus including rallies where **Player A** is a server as well as those where it is **Player B**. However, according to the **TTN**, the tactics used by a player in a rally strongly depend on whether this player is serving or receiving for this rally. This is why we have reapplied our method on a reduced dataset only composed of rallies where one of the two players is serving. Best **Player A**'s tactics when **Player A** is serving are represented in Table 3. The other configurations, such as best **Player A**'s tactics when **Player B** serves, and similar results for **Player B**'s tactics are given in Appendix A.

Table 3. Best **Player A**'s tactics when **Player A** is server.

WRAcc	Frequency	Winrate	Player A's Stroke	Player B's Stroke	Player A's Stroke
0.05024	16.4%	88.9%	Forehand R_ss, M1	Forehand Push	Forehand
0.03967	18.2%	80.0%	Forehand R_ss	Forehand Push	Forehand Attack
0.03041	7.3%	100.0%	R3	Backhand	Forehand Attack, R3
0.02744	10.9%	83.3%	Forehand	Control	Backhand Control
0.03802	5.5%	100.0%	Backhand, R3	Backhand	Forehand Attack, R3

These tactics seem to be more relevant because of their higher WRAcc. For example, Table 3 shows that **Player A**'s best tactic when serving is to start with a right side serve in M1. Thus, this serve tends to force **Player B** to do a push, which allows **Player A** to take the lead.

In order to compare them, we can also look at the losing tactics by selecting tactics with the worst WRAcc in each case. Worst **Player A**'s tactics when he serve are given in Table 4 and the other configuration in Appendix A.

Table 4. Worst **Player A**'s tactics when **Player A** is server.

WRAcc	Frequency	Winrate	Player A's Stroke	Player B's Stroke	Player A's Stroke
−0.09355	25.0%	21.4%	R_ss	Forehand	L3
−0.06347	10.9%	0.0%	Forehand R_ss, M2	Forehand	Control, M3
−0.05289	9.1%	0.0%	Forehand R_ss, M2	Attack	Control

In contrast to the right side serve in M1, Table 4 shows that tactics starting with a right side serve in M2 are losing for **Player A**. This is because the M2 service is risky. Indeed, the objective of this serve is to be short enough so that the opponent cannot make an offensive stoke but long enough so that it is difficult to make a push. According to Table 4 line 3, **Player B** made offensive returns on this serve, which means that **Player A** made too long serves in M2. To get a better idea of how **Player A** uses these tactics, we can look at the evolution of the use of these different serves in Fig. 4.

Figure 4 presents the types of serves used during the match: on the ordinate we have the types of serves and on the abscissa the rallies ordered in time. The

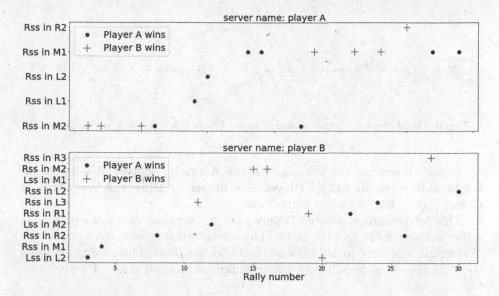

Fig. 4. Evolution of the serves used by **Player A** and **Player B**.

color of each point identifies the winner of each rally. On Fig. 4, we can highlight the fact that **Player A** started the game with a risky strategy by using right side serves in M2. However, as seen in Fig. 4 and Table 4, this strategy was not successful. **Player A** then used right side serves in M1 from the 7th rally. It was a less risky serve that allowed him to regain the advantage over **Player B**.

3.2   Visualization of the Tactics

To explore data and visualize subgroups discovered through data mining, we can use the graph representation of rallies described in Sect. 2.1. Examples of this representation are given for the tactics analyzed in Sect. 3.1.

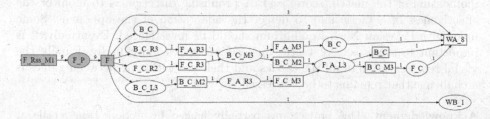

Fig. 5. Graph representation of best **Player A**'s tactic when he serves.

Figure 5 represents the following **Player A**'s tactic : **Player A's forehand Right-side serve in M1** → **Player B's Forehand Push** → **Player A's forehand**. This corresponds to the first tactic in Table 3.

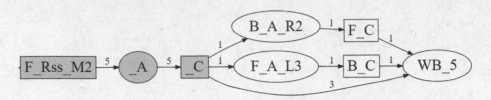

Fig. 6. Graph representation of one of worst **Player A**'s tactic when he serves.

Figure 6 represents the following **Player A**'s tactic: **Player A's forehand Right-side serve in M2 → Player A's attack → Player A's control**. It corresponds to the second tactic in Table 4.

This representation allows to easily read the sequence of strokes present in rallies containing the selected tactic. This visualization reflects the risky nature of the right side serve in M2 because the rallies are short, while the tactic using the right side serve in M1 gives longer rallies, although it allows **Player A** to take the lead.

4   Conclusion and Perspectives

We have introduced some preliminary results for discovering and visualizing tactics in a single Table Tennis game, based on subgroup discovery. Given Tennis Table data, we show that it is possible to discover some tactics that have a positive impact on the score of the player (i.e., the fraction of points that are won increases). We believe that such method can support knowledge discovery from Tennis Table games and provide insights for both the players and their coaches. However, a number of potential limitations need to be considered for future research to make this method effective in practice. First, a tactic – no matter how effective it is – must be used wisely. If a tactic is always used by a player, the opponent will adapt and its effectiveness will decrease through the game. It is therefore important to provide more context to a tactic (e.g., momentum of the match, score, set). A promising direction is to monitor the effectiveness of a tactic and to detect the adaptation of the opponent. Some links with Bayesian Nash Equilibrium should be investigated. Eventually, it is important to study sets of tactics instead of tactics individually. Finally the visual representation of all the tactics and their use within or between games is a challenge that remains to be addressed.

Acknowledgment. This project was partially funded by Action Transversale at LIRIS Lab. We thank **Table Tennis National partner** for the annotated game they provided us and their time to provide us with feedback on the results. We also thank the reviewers for their thoughtful comments.

A   Appendix

Table 5. Best **Player A**'s tactics when **Player B** is server.

WRAcc	Frequency	Winrate	Player A's Stroke	Player B's Stroke	Player A's Stroke
0.05340	11.3%	100.0%	Push	Forehand Push	Attack
0.04450	9.4%	100.0%	Backhand Push	Forehand Push	Attack
0.04450	9.4%	100.0%	Push, M1	Forehand	Backhand
0.03560	13.2%	85.7%	Backhand	Forehand	Backhand Attack
0.03560	7.5%	100.0%	Backhand Push	Forehand Push	Backhand Attack

Table 6. Best **Player B**'s tactics when **Player B** is server.

WRAcc	Frequency	Winrate	Player B's Stroke	Player A's Stroke	Player B's Stroke
0.05981	11.3%	100.0%	R3	Forehand Control	Forehand
0.05304	20.8%	72.7%	Forehand	Control	Attack
0.04984	9.4%	100.0%	Forehand, R3	Forehand Control	Forehand
0.04984	9.4%	100.0%	Forehand	Forehand Control	Attack
0.04984	9.4%	100.0%	Attack	Forehand Control	Forehand

Table 7. Best **Player B**'s tactics when **Player A** is server.

WRAcc	Frequency	Winrate	Player B's Stroke	Player A's Stroke	Player B's Stroke
0.03471	9.1%	80.0%	Control	Attack, L3	Forehand
0.03174	5.4%	100.0%	Control	Backhand Attack, M3	Backhand Control
0.03174	5.4%	100.0%	Attack	Backhand Control	Attack
0.02711	10.9%	66.7%	Backhand	L3	Forehand
0.02413	7.3%	75.0%	Backhand Control	Backhand Attack	Control

Table 8. Worst **Player A**'s tactics when **Player B** is server.

WRAcc	Frequency	Winrate	Player A's Stroke	Player B's Stroke	Player A's Stroke
−0.09078	20.8%	9.1%	Control	Attack	Control, R3
−0.08971	17.0%	0.0%	M3	Forehand	R3
−0.08188	22.6%	16.7%	Control	Attack	Control

Table 9. Worst **Player B**'s tactics when **Player B** is server.

WRAcc	Frequency	Winrate	Player B's Stroke	Player A's Stroke	Player B's Stroke
−0.09790	20.8%	0.0%	Forehand	Forehand	M1
−0.09683	23.6%	7.7%	Forehand	Attack	L3
−0.09576	27.3%	13.3%	Forehand	Forehand	Backhand, M3

Table 10. Worst **Player B**'s tactics when **Player A** is server.

WRAcc	Frequency	Winrate	Player B's Stroke	Player A's Stroke	Player B's Stroke
−0.05322	12.7%	0.0%	Backhand	Attack, R3	M3
−0.04562	10.9%	0.0%	Forehand Push	Forehand	Control, R3
−0.04562	10.9%	0.0%	Forehand Push	Control	Control, R3

References

1. Atzmueller, M.: Subgroup discovery. Wiley Interdisc. Rev. Data Min. Knowl. Disc. **5**(1), 35–49 (2015)
2. Decroos, T., Haaren, J.V., Davis, J.: Automatic discovery of tactics in spatio-temporal soccer match data. In: Proceedings of the 24th ACM SIGKDD International Conference on Knowledge Discovery and Data Mining, pp. 223–232. Association for Computing Machinery (2018)
3. Fournier-Viger, P., Gomariz, A., Campos, M., Thomas, R.: Fast vertical mining of sequential patterns using co-occurrence information. In: Tseng, V.S., Ho, T.B., Zhou, Z.-H., Chen, A.L.P., Kao, H.-Y. (eds.) PAKDD 2014. LNCS (LNAI), vol. 8443, pp. 40–52. Springer, Cham (2014). https://doi.org/10.1007/978-3-319-06608-0_4
4. Kralj Novak, P., Lavrač, N., Webb, G.I.: Supervised descriptive rule discovery: a unifying survey of contrast set, emerging pattern and subgroup mining. J. Mach. Learn. Res. **10**, 377–403 (2009)
5. Mathonat, R., Nurbakova, D., Boulicaut, J.-F., Kaytoue, M.: SeqScout: using a bandit model to discover interesting subgroups in labeled sequences. In: 2019 IEEE International Conference on Data Science and Advanced Analytics (DSAA), pp. 81–90 (Oct 2019)
6. Müller, M.: Dynamic time warping. information retrieval for music and motion. Inf. Retrieval Music Motion **2**, 69–84 (2007)
7. Wang, J., Wu, J., Cao, A., Zhou, Z., Zhang, H., Wu, Y.: Tac-Miner: visual tactic mining for multiple table tennis matches. IEEE Trans. Vis. Comput. Graph. **27**(6), 2770–2782 (2021). Conference Name: IEEE Transactions on Visualization and Computer Graphics
8. Wang, J., et al.: Tac-Simur: tactic-based Simulative visual analytics of table tennis. IEEE Trans. Vis. Comput. Graph. **26**(1), 407–417 (2020). Conference Name: IEEE Transactions on Visualization and Computer Graphics
9. Wu, Y.: et al.: iTTVis: interactive visualization of table tennis data. IEEE Trans. Vis. Comput. Graph. **24**(1), 709–718 (2018). Conference Name: IEEE Transactions on Visualization and Computer Graphics

Cycling

Athlete Monitoring in Professional Road Cycling Using Similarity Search on Time Series Data

Arie-Willem de Leeuw[1]([⊠]), Tobias Oberkofler[2], Mathieu Heijboer[3], and Arno Knobbe[2]

[1] Department of Computer Science, University of Antwerp - imec, Antwerp, Belgium
arie-willem.deleeuw@uantwerpen.be
[2] Leiden Institute of Advanced Computer Science (LIACS), Leiden, The Netherlands
[3] Team Jumbo-Visma, 's-Hertogenbosch, The Netherlands

Abstract. In sports, athlete monitoring is important for preventing injuries and optimizing performance. The multitude of relevant factors during the exercise sessions, such as weather conditions, makes proper individual athlete monitoring labour intensive. In this work, we develop an automated approach for athlete monitoring in professional road cycling that takes into account the terrain on which the ride is executed by finding segments with similar elevation profiles. In our approach, the matching is focused on the shapes of the segments. We use 2.5 years of data of a single rider of Team Jumbo-Visma and assess the performance of our approach by determining the quality of the best matches for a selection of 700 distinct segments, consisting of the most representative shapes for the elevation profiles. We demonstrate that the execution time is within seconds and more than ten times faster than exhaustive search. Therefore, our method enables real-time deployment in large scale applications with potentially many requests from multiple users. Moreover, we show that on average our approach has similar accuracy when considering the correlation to a target segment and approximately only has a twice as large mean squared error when compared to exhaustive search. Finally, we discuss a practical example to demonstrate how our approach can be used for athlete performance monitoring.

Keywords: Sports analytics · Data mining · Time series data · Road cycling

1 Introduction

Over the last decades, technical developments have led to new opportunities for detailed athlete monitoring in sports. Here, the main focus is on tracking the fatigue from exercising and the corresponding recovery. In particular, the aim is finding the right balance between training stress and recovery on

This work is part of the Nationale SportInnovatorprijs 2020 *WielerFitheid*, which is financed by ZonMW.

an athlete-specific level [13]. Monitoring this balance has two main benefits for sports practitioners. First, if training programs contain insufficient recovery, this can result in severe injuries. Therefore, detailed monitoring could signal early symptoms of potentially severe injuries that might occur in the future [18]. Second, the performance of athletes can be enhanced by tracking the adaptions of the body after completing a training session. Hence, coaches keep an eye on their athletes on a daily basis to optimize performance and prevent injuries [7,11].

For a coach, athlete monitoring is a complicated task as there is a multitude of different factors that need to be considered, such as the characteristics of training sessions or the wellness of an athlete [29]. Hereby, it is crucial to interpret the findings by taking into account the right contextual information. For example, an elevated heart rate during a training session could be explained by a higher body temperature due to environmental factors [15]. Additionally, there is a potential risk of missing possible relevant information in the often vast amounts of collected data. As coaches are usually responsible for a group of athletes who all need an individualized analysis, athlete monitoring is labour intensive and one of the most important daily occupations of a coach. Hence, there is a need for efficient and easy-to-implement athlete monitoring methods that can assist coaches in retrieving the most valuable information [21].

Road cycling is a prime example of a sport with many opportunities for developing these automated approaches in athlete monitoring [26]. Bikes of cyclists are typically equipped with multiple sensors and therefore detailed information of the bike rides is available. This collection of ample sensor data opens up many avenues to apply machine learning techniques in elite cycling [12,17,30]. In this work, we will consider an application of machine learning techniques that uses sensor data in road cycling to develop an approach for comparing the performance of a cyclist in different training sessions. In particular, for a given part of a bike ride, we automatically find other bike rides on a similar terrain and compare the physiological characteristics, such as the relationship between heart rate and produced power. By monitoring possible changes in the physiological characteristics of the rider between both bike rides taking place on distinct dates, our method can assist in signaling the physical development of cyclists.

The remainder of this article is structured as follows. First, we review some related work. Hereafter, we discuss the materials that are considered in this work and elaborate on the modeling approach that we have developed. Subsequently, we present the results of experiments on the performance of our approach and give an example of a typical outcome. Finally, we discuss our results and end with a conclusion.

2 Related Work

In this work, we are dealing with time series data. This type of data is omnipresent in multiple domains covering climate studies as well as finance and medicine research. Therefore, there is a large variety in time series data analyses [9,10,14], such as forecasting, classification or regression settings. Here, we consider the task of finding the part of a time series that is similar to a given segment of distinct time series. So, we are in the research area of time series similarity or matching of time series [16].

There are many approaches for addressing matching of time series, ranging from naive brute force methods to statistical analysis and deep representation learning. Most approaches rely on dimensionality reduction of the time series data using techniques such as Discrete Fourier Transform [2], Discrete Wavelet Transform [6] or t-SNE [20]. More recently, the UMAP algorithm [5] is also applied to map single and multi-attribute biomedical time series data, into a lower-dimensional feature space [4]. After the dimensionality reduction, the similarity of time series can be assessed by comparing their key characteristics.

The time series can also be matched by calculating a distance measure between entire time series [8]. Here, the most common approach is a point-by-point comparison of the absolute distance by using the Euclidean distance [31]. Alternatively, the similarity can be determined by using Dynamic Time Warping [25], or by solely focusing on the shape of the time series [3]. After obtaining the distance between a collection of time series, there are two main options for determining the similarity between time series [16]. First, given a time series T, we can explore a database to retrieve all other time series that are within a predefined threshold distance of T. Second, clustering approaches can be applied to find the groups of similar time series. For example, k-mediods clustering with the Dynamic Time Warping distance can be used [22]. An overview of the various approaches of time series clustering can be found in Refs. [1,19].

3 Materials

In this section, we will describe the materials that are used in the study and elaborate on the preprocession that we have applied.

3.1 Materials

We consider 2.5 years of training and competition data of an elite cyclist of Team Jumbo-Visma. During the rides, many attributes are collected by using sensors and a bike computer. We have physiological attributes, such as the produced power and heart rate, and also environmental information, including the location and altitude of the terrain. In total, the rider completed almost 800 sessions. The data of each session is a time series, where the information is collected with a resolution 1 Hz. Ignoring sessions with malfunction of the bike computer, such as a session shorter than 1 km, we find that the average length and duration of a session is 95.6 ± 56.9 km and 179 ± 95.6 min (mean $\pm$ std), respectively.

3.2 Data Preprocessing

Before using the data in our modeling approaches, we first apply some prepro-cessing. In this step, we developed a pipeline to remove outliers, inconsistent data

Fig. 1. The seven main distinct shape types that can be encountered when investigating the elevation profile of road cycling rides.

points and missing values. Most importantly, we applied Gaussian smoothing on the altitude variable to overcome the step-wise increase of the altitude values in the raw data. After exploring different values of the standard deviation of the Gaussian kernel, we set $\sigma = 3$ to remove the discontinuous behavior and in the meantime preserve most fluctuations. Moreover, segments with less than 60 s of consecutive missing values, are filled by applying spline interpolation. Finally, we down-sampled the original one Hertz data to a 15 s sampling rate. Although we hereby remove some details, the precision is sufficient to retrieve accurate information for our road cycling application.

4   Methodology

The goal of our work is to retrieve core information between comparable ride segments in different recorded sessions of a given rider. More specifically, we consider the following challenge

Given: A segment S defined as a specific part of an entire workout that is of arbitrary length, selected from a collection of time series, and of the form $\{(d_s, h_s), \ldots, (d_f, h_f)\}$. Here, d_j is the covered distance, h_j is the corresponding altitude, and the indices s and f correspond to the first and last point of the segment, respectively.

Goal: Find the segments that are conditioned on similar terrain, i.e., have a similar elevation profile compared to S.

As mentioned previously in the related work section, there are several options for addressing this task. For practical usage, our approach should be sufficiently fast while minimizing the risks of missing relevant matches. Here, we need to meet this requirement for all different types of elevation profiles. After inspection of all time series data in our database, we find that an elevation profile is typically equal to one of the seven different kind of shapes shown in Fig. 1.

In this work, we have applied two different approaches that are accurate and fast enough for all distinct elevation profiles. Before we will elaborate on these two procedures in more detail, we first discuss an additional step that both approaches have in common.

4.1   Selection of Potential Matches

For our methods to be sufficiently fast, it is unfeasible to take a naive approach and perform a comparison to all other segments of the same length. Note that this is also unnecessary as the characteristics of most of these segments will be quite different. Therefore, we determine general properties of the selected segment S and preselect potential matches by imposing conditions on these characteristics.

First, we determine the extreme points in altitude of segment S. Next, we define a minimum and maximum allowed altitude that is 10% lower or higher, respectively. Hereafter, we consider all segments of the same length as S and select the ones for which at all time points, the altitude is in between the minimum and maximum allowed altitude. Subsequently, we filter out matches with a Pearson's correlation of less than 0.7 with the query segment.

4.2   Taylor-made Approach

After selecting the potential matches, we can apply our approaches for finding similar segments to S. In our first method, we use a similarity measure to determine the similarity between the segment S and the potential matches.

In principle, there are multiple similarity measures that can be applied. For optimizing the usability for sport practitioners in this specific use case, an agreement in shape of the segments is most important. Moreover, in the selection of potential matches, we already ensured that the altitude values are in the same range by restricting the difference between altitude in both segments and enforcing a minimal correlation between them. Therefore, we have chosen the *peak alignment* as our similarity measure, which closely corresponds to human judgment of mountainous terrain in cycling. With the peak alignment, we match the identified peaks between two series in sequential order and compute the sum of weighted horizontal differences between the summits. The differences are weighted by the summits relative altitude that is defined as the absolute altitude of the summit divided by the sessions maximum altitude. Although here we focus on the objective of peak alignment, the approach can be easily extended to allow for different (combinations) of evaluation metrics.

We use the scipy signal package[1] to identify peaks. If there are no clear peaks in the original segment, such as sprints or simple climbs, the Pearson correlation coefficient is used as similarity score. Finally, we sort all matches from most to least similar and remove overlapping segments to ensure variety in the results.

4.3   Dimensionality Reduction Approach

In our second approach, we utilize techniques of dimensionality reduction to project the time series into low dimensional space and apply a k-nearest neighbour (KNN) classification to identify the most similar segments for any given segment S. In principle, dimensional reduction can be quite time-consuming, as there is a need for extensive preprocessing and the buffering for non-linear reduction methods requires a huge memory. From a practical perspective, it is often not feasible to use this approach if dimensionality reduction has to be performed for each new query. However, in the case of fixed sized windows, the

---

[1] https://docs.scipy.org/doc/scipy/reference/generated/scipy.signal.find_peaks.html.

computational complexity reduces to a $\mathcal{O}(1)$ lookup operation at execution time. In this case, the dimensionality reduction only has to be performed once and the results can be stored and retrieved on demand. We experimented with different forms of dimension reduction such as UMAP, t-SNE and Principal Component Analysis (PCA). For efficiency reasons, we here opt for PCA.

Before performing the dimensionality reduction, we add the slope of the terrain as additional feature to the original time series data. Hereafter, we apply normalization of the features and learn an n-dimensional representation of segments with a given length k. We project all sub-parts of our data collection with length k into the low-dimensional space and determine the nearest neighbours with the Euclidean distance measure. The value of n is determined by using a representative sample of different distance altitude segments for a given k, and evaluating the average top-5 mean-squared-error as well as the correlation to the target segment.

Although less efficient when not restricted to segments of fixed length, this approach also has an advantage compared to the first method. If we apply an n-dimensional reduction of segments for $n < 4$, we can visualise the characteristics of all segments of a given length k that are present in our data collection. Thereby, we can explore all different type of segments and also find potential clusters of similar fragments. Hence, the user can visually explore the landscape of all available segments and find the similar segments without specifying one specific segment S in advance.

5   Results

In this section, we will present the assessment of the performance of our modeling approaches and illustrate how our approach can be used for athlete monitoring.

5.1   Modeling Performance

To obtain realistic estimates of the performance of our approaches under real-world conditions, we present the results of experiments on a sample of 700 manually selected segments of about 1 h length equally representing the 7 distinct shape types displayed in Fig. 1. The experiments are executed on a machine with 32×8-core Intel(R) Xeon(R) CPU E5-2630-v3 central processing units with a combined RAM of 440 GB using parallel creation and comparison of the sliding segment-windows.

Before we can compare our methods, we first need to find the optimal number of components in our dimensionality reduction approach. After investigating the performance on a log-2 scale, we find that the optimal number of components is around 2^4. However, for more than 2^2 components the performance, defined as the average correlation and mean squared error, only marginally increases. We find that representations with 2- or 3-dimensions already result in compelling clusters which can be used for visualization.

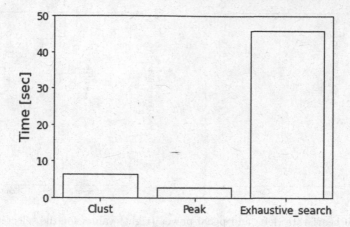

Fig. 2. Computation time for finding the three best matches for 100 segments of each of the 7 distinct shape types of Fig. 1. We display the average computation time for our taylor made approach (peak), dimensional reduction (clust) approach and exhaustive search.

We assess the performance of our method by investigating the computation time and accuracy of our different approaches. In Fig. 2, we show the average time necessary for finding the three best matches. We observe that exhaustive search has the largest computational time. This method takes more than ten times longer than our taylor-made approach, which on average needs under three seconds to obtain the three best matches for a given segment S. The overall quality of the matches is displayed in Fig. 3. We observe that the overall quality of retrieved matches is very high with an average Pearson's correlation around 0.85 and mean squared error smaller than 120m altitude for all methods. The Pearson's correlation of all methods is comparable, while the exhaustive search method has a mean squared error that is approximately two times smaller than

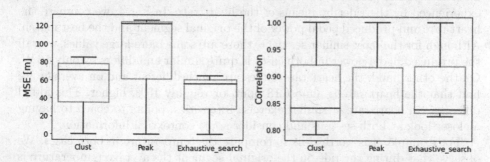

Fig. 3. Comparison of the accuracy of our taylor made approach (peak), dimensional reduction (clust) approach and exhaustive search. We show the distribution of the mean squared error (left) and Pearson's correlation (right) for experiments on a total 700 segments where all 7 different shape types of Fig. 1 are equally represented.

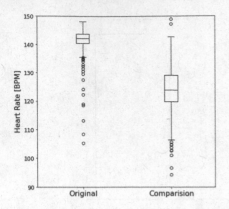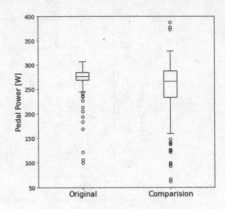

Fig. 4. The heart rate (left) and pedal power (right) values for the selected segment and the best match. We observe there is quite a difference in heart rate values although the produced power in both cases in similar.

our taylor-made approach. Note that we combined the results for all distinct shapes of the elevation profiles, but we obtain similar results if we consider the distinct shapes separately.

5.2   Athlete Monitoring

As an illustration of the usefulness of our approach, we consider of one session the El Teide climb in Spain with starting point in Chio. This case is of particular interest for the coaches as this is a popular training location for cyclists. For this example, we find that the best match is a different climb on Tenerife. Moreover, the top-5 matches for the given query segment all have a Pearson's correlation coefficient above 0.99 and a mean-squared error difference smaller than 50 m.

To obtain interesting insights for athlete monitoring, we analyze the exercise intensity via the produced pedal power and relate this to the heaviness that is experienced by the rider by means of the heart rate. In Fig. 4, we compare the heart rate and produced pedal power of the original segment and the best match. Although for the most similar segment, there are some more large values, overall the produced pedal power in both cases is quite similar and differs by only 16 W. On the other hand, the heart rate values are much different and on average, we find that the heart rate is almost 18 bpm, or roughly 15%, higher. This found difference in heart rate at similar exercise intensities, points to coach to having a closer look at both sessions and consider some contextual information.

For example, it is worthwhile to compare the temperature in both cases. We observe that during the ride on the original segment the average temperature is almost 8 °C lower than during the compared session. This might indicate that the temperature difference could be the explanation for the observed dissimilarity in heart rate. We can further investigate this claim by comparing the second best match to the original segment. In this case, we have a comparable difference in temperature as found before. Moreover, compared to the original segment, the average heart rate is 8 bpm lower and on average the cyclist produced 28 W less power. Hence, there is a larger difference in produced pedal power, but the heart rate is more similar. Therefore, this suggests that the difference in heart rate as shown in Fig. 4 can not only be caused by the change in temperature. In a similar fashion a coach could consider other contextual information, such as the run-up to the segment in both rides. Hereby, it is possible to study whether the observed difference in heart rate at similar produced pedal power was a consequence of a change in fitness of the rider or there was another explanation.

6   Discussion

We have presented three approaches for finding similar elevation profiles in professional road cycling. Although exhaustive search is most accurate, there is only a relatively small gain compared to our other two approaches, especially in terms of the correlation metric. On the other hand, exhaustive search often takes over a minute to find results and our taylor-made method retrieves comparable results in under three seconds. This demonstrates that this approach is suitable for any real-time deployment if the application needs to be scaled up to a service with multiple simultaneous requests.

Thereafter, we illustrated the usefulness of our approach by considering a practical example. Although the races were executed on similar terrain and the exercise intensities were comparable, we observed that there were significant differences in heart rate that could not be explained by only looking at the temperature difference in both sessions. This elevated heart rate at the same exercise intensity could indicate a decrease in performance [32] or a reduction in training volume [23,24] at the original segment. However, before drawing these conclusions, it is important that the coach also takes into account all contextual information. For example, the exercise intensity and exercise duration before starting the segment could have been different. Therefore, it would be worthwhile to extend our approach by including some restrictions, such as enforcing similar physiological starting conditions. For instance, the energy used until the starting point of a segment could by calculated by determining the work done up until starting the segment.

In addition to the application of our method for athlete monitoring, we have another useful utilization for sport practitioners in road cycling. Instead of finding the most similar segment in historical data, we can also use the elevation profile of a future race. In this case, we can select parts that are expected to be important for the race outcome and use our approach to find similar segments in our data collection. Hereby, we can determine specific areas in popular training destinations that have a similar elevation profile. This can be an asset in the build-up for important races as this allows riders to experience the terrain of the race, without the additional need for travelling to the specific location.

There are multiple opportunities for future research. As mentioned before, for athlete monitoring it can be important to extend our approach and include some restrictions on the matches. Moreover, it is interesting to investigate multiple riders as this also allows for comparison of the physiological characteristics between different riders. Finally, we can also explore alternatives for some choices that we have made in our approach. For instance, we have preselected candidate segments based on the extreme values of the altitude of the target segment and the Pearson's correlation. These specific choices are most appropriate for segments that include high altitudes and sufficient elevation differences. On the other hand, a preselection based on absolute errors between the elevation profiles might be more reliable for segments that contain little elevation differences. While the segments with large altitude difference are the most important for coaches as these are typically very demanding for cyclists, it also might be insightful to accurately compare other type of segments. Therefore, an extension of our approach could be a more flexible procedure for the preselection of potential matches that is based on the characteristics of the target segment. Finally, we could also apply different approaches, such as hierarchical clustering [27], or clustering based on Dynamic Time Warping Barycenter Averaging [28].

7   Conclusion

In this work, we have developed methods for athlete monitoring in professional road cycling. We obtained insights about the physical abilities and fatigue of a professional road cyclist by finding similar elevation profiles of bike rides. Our main approach uses multi-stage filtering and peak alignment to assess this similarity, which is most in line with the human perception if segments are alike. We have shown that this approach is sufficiently accurate and fast to allow for real-time application. In addition to comparing the physiological characteristics of a rider between segments with similar elevation profiles occurring on different dates, our approach can also be used to prepare for future races by identifying areas in training locations with similar terrain as a given future race. Concluding, we have constructed a valuable tool for sport practitioners in professional road cycling that can be used for efficient and effective athlete monitoring to support performance optimization.

References

1. Aghabozorgi, S., Shirkhorshidi, A.S., Wah, T.Y.: Time-series clustering-a decade review. Inf. Syst. **53**, 16–38 (2015)
2. Agrawal, R., Faloutsos, C., Swami, A.: Efficient similarity search in sequence databases. In: Lomet, D.B. (ed.) FODO 1993. LNCS, vol. 730, pp. 69–84. Springer, Heidelberg (1993). https://doi.org/10.1007/3-540-57301-1_5
3. Agrawal, R., Lin, K.I., Sawhney, H.S., Shim, K.: Fast similarity search in the presence of noise, scaling, and translation in time-series databases. In: Proceedings of the 21th International Conference on Very Large Data Bases. VLDB 1995, San Francisco, CA, USA, pp. 490–501. Morgan Kaufmann Publishers Inc. (1995)

4. Ali, M., Jones, M.W., Xie, X., Williams, M.: Timecluster: dimension reduction applied to temporal data for visual analytics. Vis. Comput. **35**(6), 1013–1026 (2019)
5. Becht, E., et al.: Dimensionality reduction for visualizing single-cell data using UMAP. Nat. Biotechnol. **37**(1), 38–44 (2019)
6. pong Chan, K., Fu, A.W.C.: Efficient time series matching by wavelets. In: Proceedings 15th International Conference on Data Engineering (Cat. No.99CB36337), pp. 126–133 (1999)
7. Coutts, A., Cormack, S.: Monitoring the training response. High-performance training for sports, pp. 71–84 (2014)
8. Ding, H., Trajcevski, G., Scheuermann, P., Wang, X., Keogh, E.: Querying and mining of time series data: experimental comparison of representations and distance measures. Proc. VLDB Endowment **1**(2), 1542–1552 (2008)
9. Esling, P., Agon, C.: Time-series data mining. ACM Comput. Surv. **45**(1) (2012). https://doi.org/10.1145/2379776.2379788
10. Fakhrazari, A., Vakilzadian, H.: A survey on time series data mining. In: 2017 IEEE International Conference on Electro Information Technology, EIT 2017, pp. 476–481. IEEE International Conference on Electro Information Technology, IEEE Computer Society (Sep 2017). DOI: https://doi.org/10.1109/EIT.2017.8053409,2017 IEEE International Conference on Electro Information Technology, EIT 2017; Conference date: 14-05-2017 Through 17-05-2017
11. Halson, S.L.: Monitoring training load to understand fatigue in athletes. Sports Med. **44**(2), 139–147 (2014)
12. Hilmkil, A., Ivarsson, O., Johansson, M., Kuylenstierna, D., van Erp, T.: Towards machine learning on data from professional cyclists. arXiv preprint arXiv:1808.00198 (2018)
13. Kellmann, M.: Preventing overtraining in athletes in high-intensity sports and stress/recovery monitoring. Scandinavian J. Med. Sci. Sports **20**, 95–102 (2010)
14. Keogh, E., Kasetty, S.: On the need for time series data mining benchmarks: a survey and empirical demonstration. Data Mining Knowl. Discov. **7**(4), 349–371 (2003). https://doi.org/10.1023/A:1024988512476
15. Kirschen, G.W., Singer, D.D., Thode, H.C., Jr., Singer, A.J.: Relationship between body temperature and heart rate in adults and children: a local and national study. Am. J. Emerg. Med. **38**(5), 929–933 (2020)
16. Kontaki, M., Papadopoulos, A., Manolopoulos, Y.: Similarity search in time series databases (2006). https://doi.org/10.4018/9781591405603.ch106
17. de Leeuw, A.-W., Heijboer, M., Hofmijster, M., van der Zwaard, S., Knobbe, A.: Time series regression in professional road cycling. In: Appice, A., Tsoumakas, G., Manolopoulos, Y., Matwin, S. (eds.) DS 2020. LNCS (LNAI), vol. 12323, pp. 689–703. Springer, Cham (2020). https://doi.org/10.1007/978-3-030-61527-7_45
18. de Leeuw, A.W., van der Zwaard, S., van Baar, R., Knobbe, A.: Personalized machine learning approach to injury monitoring in elite volleyball players. Eur. J. Sport Sci. **22**, 511–520 (2021)
19. Liao, T.W.: Clustering of time series data-a survey. Pattern Recogn. **38**(11), 1857–1874 (2005)
20. Van der Maaten, L., Hinton, G.: Visualizing data using T-SNE. J. Mach. Learn. Res. **9**(11) (2008)
21. McGuigan, H., Hassmén, P., Rosic, N., Stevens, C.: Monitoring of training in high-performance athletes: what do practitioners do? J. Sci. Sport Exerc. **5**, 121–129 (2021). https://doi.org/10.36905/jses.2021.02.05

22. Meert, W., Hendrickx, K., Craenendonck, T.V.: wannesm/dtaidistance v2. 0.0. Zenodo (2020)
23. Mujika, I., Padilla, S.: Detraining: loss of training-induced physiological and performance adaptations. Part I: short term insufficient training stimulus. Sports Med. **30**(2), 79–87 (2000). https://doi.org/10.2165/00007256-200030020-00002
24. Mujika, I., Padilla, S.: Detraining: loss of training-induced physiological and performance adaptations. Part II: Long term insufficient training stimulus. Sports Med. **30**(3), 145–54 (2000). https://doi.org/10.2165/00007256-200030030-00001
25. Müller, M.: Dynamic Time Warping. In: Information Retrieval for Music and Motion, pp. 69–84. Springer, Heidelberg (2007). https://doi.org/10.1007/978-3-540-74048-3_4
26. Municio, E., et al.: Continuous athlete monitoring in challenging cycling environments using IoT technologies. IEEE Internet Things J. **6**(6), 10875–10887 (2019)
27. Nielsen, F.: Hierarchical Clustering, pp. 195–211 (02 2016)
28. Petitjean, F., Ketterlin, A., Gançarski, P.: A global averaging method for dynamic time warping, with applications to clustering. Pattern Recogn. **44**(3), 678–693 (2011)
29. Saw, A.E., Main, L.C., Gastin, P.B.: Monitoring the athlete training response: subjective self-reported measures trump commonly used objective measures: a systematic review. Br. J. Sports Med. **50**(5), 281–291 (2016). https://doi.org/10.1136/bjsports-2015-094758
30. Silacci, A., Taiar, R., Caon, M.: Towards an AI-based tailored training planning for road cyclists: A case study. Appl. Sci. **11**(1) (2021). https://doi.org/10.3390/app11010313
31. Soon, L.K., Lee, S.H.: An empirical study of similarity search in stock data. In: Proceedings of the 2nd International Workshop on Integrating Artificial Intelligence and Data Mining - Volume 84, pp. 31–38. AIDM 2007, Australian Computer Society Inc, AUS (2007)
32. Thorpe, R., Atkinson, G., Drust, B., Gregson, W.: Monitoring fatigue status in elite team-sport athletes: implications for practice. Int. J. Sports Physiol. Perform. **12**(Suppl 2), S227–S234 (2017). https://doi.org/10.1123/ijspp.2016-0434

Author Index

Printed in the United States
by Baker & Taylor Publisher Services